WRITING A BOOK OR THESIS
IN MICROSOFT WORD

ISBN-13: 978-1985637016

ISBN-10: 1985637014

information: www.TheFreeWindows.com

© 2018, Steven Adams

Steven Adams

Writing a book or thesis in Microsoft Word

Some important tasks and difficulties

THEFREEWINDOWS

Boston 2018

Lorem ipsum dolor, Curabitur
dolor, imperdiet
nunc ultrices leo
Curabitur cursus

Table of Contents

Preface	**11**
Enjoy real view	**13**
Ways to view your document	16
P a g e W i d t h view should be instantly available	19
100% zoom in Print Preview: make it d e f a u l t!	20
Enable magical move! Scroll your document w i t h o u t moving the cursor or mouse	21
Travel your document with Word b o o k m a r k s	22
How to create a g l o b a l bookmark, always visible, multi-present	24
Don't ignore the G o T o browser	26
Page metrics: f i r s t thing to adjust!	28
Paper size	30
Page margins	32
The Word Ribbon	34
Let your style shine!	**35**
The Normal style and template	37
How to find and modify your custom templates	41
How to create new styles	43
How to change easily any manual formatting applied here and there	45
How to export basic Word customizations	46
Resetting the Normal template without losing your customizations	47
Chapters, Sections, Headings	49
Creating Section Breaks	50
Start main chapters on o d d pages	51
Setup different headers and footers for odd and even pages	53

Let your chapters have their own distinct headers	53
Building a u t o m a t i c a l l y individual headers for your chapters	56
How to interrupt a global header	58
How to create global and unique headers in the same document	59
Odd and even headers can follow different styles	60
How to increase or decrease the distance between header (or footer) and body text	61
How to eliminate unnecessary blank space above headings	62
How to p r e s e r v e extra space above your headings	63
Prevent unnecessary horizontal lines	64
Eliminate unnecessary blank space between words when you paste	65
Page numbering can start and stop in any page	65
Page numbers at the corners	67

How to add in your text special paragraphs of n u m b e r e d l i n e s	68
Changing the case of selected text automatically and rapidly	70
Hyphenation	71
Prevent orphan l e t t e r s	72
Prevent orphan w o r d s	73

Be powerful   75

How to import your W o r d P r e s s posts	77
Importing several Word documents into your main document	77
How to split your pages vertically to put side by side two texts	78
Footnote issues	80
Open by default a larger footnotes pane in Draft view	80
Let there be columns in Footnotes!	82
Creating a Table of Contents	83
How to create multiple tables of contents in the same document	84
Toggle Field Codes View without losing focus of your current position	86
A bibliography with style	89
Creating Indexes of persons or topics	91
Index Subentries	91

Cross-references	92
Time to build your Index!	93
How to create more than one Index in the same document	94
If your Index ignores your custom font style	98
Adding Pictures	100
How to protect image quality	100
Cropping your images	101
Inserting Excel Objects	105

Publish! 107

How to check your document for errors	109
Making temporary home prints in various paper sizes	111
How to compare two documents	112
How to create a PDF version for professional publishers	114
Word and Acrobat paper size problems	116
How to insert and resize an image in Acrobat	117
Checking your final PDF for errors	117
Appendix: Word Keyboard Shortcuts	119

Preface

It's important that an author takes pleasure in writing and is ready to follow any required discipline for the benefit of the text, following inspiration and striving for clarity. Of course, the purpose of this book is not to make you a good author, but to help you find in Word a valuable tool instead of an obstacle, to enjoy using it while you become familiar with some powerful aspects of this great editor. If there existed alternatives, I would have been using them already — I do like freeware! I won't use a commercial program, if I can do my job with freeware, but I've tried all of them and there is no real alternative for Word.

The order of the main sections reflects the order an author may like to observe, but of course you should read first whatever helps you most right now or agrees with a different order you might prefer.

Assuming you enjoy some familiarity with Word, I skip functions such as how to change the style of a paragraph: the book is not for experts, but also not for absolute beginners; I'm not providing an *exhaustive* presentation of Word's abilities and disabilities.

*

Workspace comes first, in the order here suggested, how you setup Word as a convenient and inspiring environment. Workspace goes beyond that — in music, in your room's decoration... You should not neglect anything, and of course not your immediate environment inside the screen of your computer, most of all the functions of your text processor.

The second part provides instruction on the setup of a particular document, the order of certain tasks you may like to complete as you go on with your work.

The ending chapters regard printing, including your cooperation with a professional publisher such as Amazon's CreateSpace.

Everywhere emphasis is given to common mistakes and to ways of letting the program be effective, achieving easily tasks that may otherwise need a lot of time, especially when a document is large and complex.

Technical issues sometimes lead to broader topics such as aesthetics. I have worked in magazines and publishing houses, which means that, although you may finally disagree with me in some issues, you wouldn't like to disregard my views even before you know them. In any case, just use all of these as personal opinions to stimulate your own thinking and make your own decisions.

Enjoy real view

You can start writing immediately in a new document without making any adjustments at all, but my suggestion would be to decide first the size of your paper, your margins, and at least some elements of your main, "normal", style, such as the typeface you are going to use throughout your work.

D o n ' t write first, format later!

Elaborate formatting comes last or gradually, but recall Salinger's remark, how an author imagines the printed version even before writing starts! *Your workspace can inspire you or hold you back.* Choosing some basic 'looks' for your text helps to avoid the feeling of working in a mess.

You may even prefer to form the first page of your document as a temporary pseudo-cover. Word provides elegant templates, if you go to Insert > Page > Cover.

You can keep this "automatic" cover, in case you print your book in your own printer, but it won't be enough when the time comes to cooperate with a professional publisher. We'll see this in more details at the final chapters.

You might like also, even for a while, to change the background color of your document, if white has become boring. You can do this by going to Design > Page Color. This change is for your eyes only, it won't influence printing, unless you want that.[1] And you can always undo it easily, as you have to when you print with Acrobat.

> Configure the basic layout of your document trying to avoid adjustments that may 'break' later by content changes.

For instance, pictures and graphs should be inserted last. You cannot know and be certain how many pictures you really need and where to place them before you finish your text.

You will be changing this and that as you go on, yet paper size and margin size should be decided at least before you start to insert your graphics, because the exact dimensions of your images, drawings or graphs depend on that.

If you change paper and margins after you have inserted a lot of pictures, you may find yourself in trouble, having to modify the size of your pictures one by one, in case that this paper change hid a part of them or made them seem unnecessarily small, etc.

To take advantage of a stylish workspace, instead of "writing first, formatting later" think carefully and start by deciding paper size and margins, then font size and family. The following chapters may help you even on that.

---

[1] It can be adjusted in Word's Options > Display > Printing Options.

Contents of this section

Ways to view your document	16
P a g e W i d t h view should be instantly available	19
100% zoom in Print Preview: make it d e f a u l t!	20
Enable magical move! Scroll your document w i t h o u t moving the cursor or mouse	21
Travel your document with Word b o o k m a r k s	22
How to create a g l o b a l bookmark, always visible, multi-present	24
Don't ignore the G o T o browser	26
Page metrics: f i r s t thing to adjust!	28
Paper size	30
Page margins	32
The Word Ribbon	34

Ways to view your document

If your document contains several sections, you can use Outline view to examine and change its structure. You observe your book's basic structure already in the Table of Contents or by opening the Navigation Pane, but Outline view provides a unique functionality.

In Outline Word lets you select how many levels are visible, this way helping you to make temporarily invisible not only your body text but even higher levels, concentrating only to titles you want, locating sections you may need to move or edit, etc.

When you drag a title to a different location in Outline view the text follows with it, although it still remains invisible. Just don't make the mistake to move entries of your Table of Contents, if you have one and is visible, instead of the actual headings of your chapters! *To*

avoid mistakes do not ever select more levels than what you really need to work with.

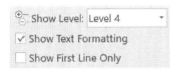

Start configuring Outline view by selecting only top headings, for instance the first 2 levels; keep adding more until you see all the headings of chapters and sections you'd like to edit or just inspect.[2]

Use Draft view when you prefer to write without caring about placement of objects on the page.

Draft view can be risky when you have graphics in your document, since some of them are invisible in this mode and you might delete them if you are careless. Draft view likes text-only versions; you can use this mode to edit easily your footnotes or even your text without viewing footnotes, to move faster in your document, etc.[3]

In Draft view the lines of a document usually flow outside your visible area! To fix this, go to Word Options > Advanced > Show document content, and activate the option, *Show text wrapped within the document window.*

---

[2] When you are in Outline view and *print* your document, Word, very rightly, prints only levels that are visible in this view, not the full text of the document.

[3] Even if you select Draft view, next time you open Word it still uses Print Layout! To change this go to Word Options > Advanced > General, and activate the option, *Allow opening a document in Draft view.*

Print Layout is what you would like and should use most of the time, since in this view Word lets you monitor on screen what you'll get in print.

A serious problem in Print Layout, especially if your vision is not perfect, is that your text may appear small compared with what you see in Draft mode.

You can solve this without sacrificing the benefits of Print Layout, by using Word's Zoom feature. This way everything may appear larger, yet with proportions remaining the same.

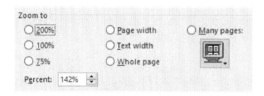

Right now I am in Print Layout using a zoom scale of 142%. Some graphics seem a little blurry, but this is not a real problem. I can monitor not only proportions but the actual size of everything when I want it, by just resorting temporarily to Print Preview mode. A keyboard shortcut activates this mode easily.[4]

---

[4] In the process of editing a document you may need several times to activate Print Preview. To use its own options (not what Word shows when you go to "Print"), assign a shortcut and / or an icon in the Quick Access Toolbar. To add an icon, go to Word Options > Quick Access Toolbar. To define a shortcut, go to Word Options > Customize Ribbon > Keyboard Shortcuts Customize > All Commands.

Page Width view should be instantly available

You open your document hungry for work, and suddenly you need to configure again your workspace! What a mess!

You know perhaps this Word annoyance. After you open several documents the program tends to forget individual zoom settings. Next time you open some of your documents, you are surprised by the loss of your favorite zoom level.

I like Page Width zoom. In this mode you can drag from a size or a corner and resize Word's window to change your zoom level instantly, without having to open the View menu, then go to Zoom, etc., to experiment with numerical values until you finally find what works for you at the moment.

To activate Page Width view easily (Word forgets even this preference!), I use a very simple macro that I assigned also to a Ribbon button.[5] You can also download it from www.TheFreeWindows.com and import it in Word to avoid typing it.

```
Sub PageWidthView()
    ActiveWindow.ActivePane.View.Zoom.PageFit = wdPageFitBestFit
End Sub
```

---

[5] You can assign it to a keyboard shortcut if you prefer but it's not necessary since you can always press *Alt + the number* that corresponds to the macro's button in the Quick Access Toolbar.

100% zoom in Print Preview: make it default!

Print Preview won't open in 100% level, it will just cover the whole window, unless you click on the page. This can become really annoying if you switch to this mode frequently, but you may add a simple macro in Word's Visual Basic Editor and assign it a keyboard shortcut (I use Ctrl + F2) to enjoy Print Preview in 100% as its default scale:

```
Sub PrintPreview100()
    With ActiveWindow.View
        .Type = wdPrintPreview
        .Zoom.Percentage = 100
    End With
End Sub
```

An easy way to open the Visual Basic Editor is to start writing its name in Word's *Command Search*. Or just press Alt + F11.

Note that sometimes when you browse your document in Print Preview mode, PageUp and PageDown may not work! You are still able to move forward pressing Ctrl+PageDown or Up, however, you wouldn't like a two-keys shortcut when a single key exists for this purpose and used to work just fine!

Your keyboard is (most probably) not mad, and you don't need to adjust any Word settings: *just try to increase the size of Word's window.* This PageDown and Up problem is caused when pages are large enough to "bleed" outside Word's window. Instead of enlarging the window, in case you don't even have enough desktop space, you can also change Zoom settings to make the preview pages smaller.

Enable magical move! Scroll your document without moving the cursor or mouse

Working with simple-text editors like Notepad++, applications that let you scroll a document without having to move the cursor, I find extremely annoying that this feature is missing from Word! To scroll in Word without moving the cursor, you have to grab the mouse and target those tiny scrollbar arrows, but this can be a pain! The alternative way, that is moving the cursor just to scroll, means you have to move it again to reach your editing location! Trouble you can so easily avoid! Personally, let me say, I can't live without this 'magical move' feature.

You don't need much to give Word mouse-free / cursor-still scrolling, just two simple macros!

I've named them (how else?) S c r o l l U p and S c r o l l D o w n...

```
Sub ScrollUp()
ActiveWindow.SmallScroll Up:=1
End Sub
```

```
Sub ScrollDown()
ActiveWindow.SmallScroll Down:=1
End Sub
```

You can copy these macros now, or just download them from www.TheFreeWindows.com and import them in Word. Then go to Word's Options > Customize > Keyboard Shortcuts, to assign any shortcuts you find convenient. I use these classical combinations: Ctrl+UpArrow to scroll upwards, and Ctrl+DownArrow to scroll downwards.

Travel your document with Word bookmarks

Authors like to change things: *everything has to be said in the best possible way*. Of course this process finds no real end, but sometime a book must finish! Until then editing and re-editing is common and welcome.

To add Word bookmarks in a document to return to certain pages, if you like to check and revise your text, just click where you want a new bookmark.

Then go to Links > Insert > Bookmark. Under *Bookmark name*, give a name that helps you to remember why you added this bookmark, such as a topic, etc., and click Add.

Note that *a bookmark name cannot have spaces*.

For instance, naming your bookmark "MS Win" won't work, you should choose a form like *MSWin*, as a single word.

Word surrounds the bookmarked item with square brackets. When you need to change this item, just edit the text or images inside these brackets and you won't lose your bookmark.[6] You may also cut, copy, and paste whole items that are marked with a bookmark.

To go to a particular bookmark's location rapidly: at the Insert tab, in the Links group, click "Bookmark" and select either Name or Location to sort your list of bookmarks. Click where you want to go to, and press the *Go To* button.

To delete a bookmark: go to Insert > Links, and click "Bookmark". Select its name and click Delete.

You can also find the Insert Bookmark command with Word's Command Search or "Tell me…"

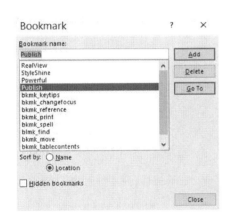

To delete both a bookmark and the bookmarked item (such as a block of text or any other element), delete the whole item.

You need to make sure you delete only bookmarks that you don't need anymore and of course not Word's *hidden* bookmarks.

---

[6] To display bookmark brackets and identify all your bookmarked locations when you browse your document, go to Options > Advanced, and at the Show document content find and select the *Show bookmarks* check box.

How to create a *global* bookmark, always visible, multi-present

Along with (or even instead of) Word's bookmarks, which you may not even need, perhaps you prefer a "super bookmark", something that you will be able to insert anywhere rapidly using just a keyboard shortcut, and find it whenever you want from whatever place in your document, using again a keyboard shortcut.

For instance, writing now this chapter, I remember suddenly a detail that I should add to the chapter about Indexes. I don't need all this process of opening Word's menus and creating a named bookmark, to leave this page and return here after a while by opening again the menus to locate and select that bookmark, which also have now to delete! I need just a temporary sign to place it here and find it immediately using a keyboard shortcut after I finish this sudden editing of my other chapter.

Here I use a few asterisks as my bookmark, but you can change it to whatever works best for you. Just make sure it's something unique in your text. You can use it multiple times and locate each instance successively using the same keyboard shortcut. It needs two macros, the first creating and the other locating it.

The first macro inserts your bookmark:

```
Sub CreateBookmark()
    Selection.TypeText Text:="******************"
End Sub
```

The second macro finds your bookmark:

```
Sub GoToBookmark()
    Application.EnableCancelKey = xlDisabled
    Selection.Find.ClearFormatting
    Selection.Find.Replacement.ClearFormatting
    With Selection.Find
        .Text = "*******************"
        .Replacement.Text = ""
        .Forward = True
        .Wrap = wdFindContinue
        .Format = False
        .MatchCase = False
        .MatchWholeWord = False
        .MatchWildcards = False
        .MatchSoundsLike = False
        .MatchAllWordForms = False
    End With
    Selection.Find.Execute
End Sub
```

You can download both macros from www.TheFreeWindows.com to import them easily in Word. Assign to each of them a keyboard shortcut.

If you place these macros in the Quick Access Toolbar, you will be able to insert and find your bookmark with the mouse, while simultaneously you will have assigned to each of them an Alt+SomeNumber keyboard shortcut.

An author needs to handle lots of things unexpectedly; this "super bookmark" provides a very simple, and really fast and flexible way to mark one or several locations to leave and return whenever you want without hesitation.

Don't ignore the Go To browser

If your document is divided by a lot of sections or includes a great number of graphics or other special items or locations, you may need to find some or all of these to check for errors, for omissions or even just to refresh your memory and gain some inspiration.

There is a pleasure in browsing the whole book page by page, but how many times? If you are doing it for the fiftieth time, perhaps you'd like now to concentrate on a particular task and leave for later the browsing of the whole book, when partial editing is over or almost over and you are ready to let your final version be published!

Word offers this great tool for doing your job.

Press Ctrl + G and your familiar *Find and Replace* panel opens in the "Go To" tab.

If you don't remember the keyboard shortcut, you can just type "Find" in the familiar Command Search box at the ribbon, and go to *Find & Select > Go to*.

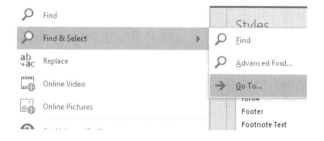

Go To provides a list of objects, common destinations that are available if you need to locate them easily.

Select an item you're interested in, and press the "Next" button.

Keep pressing "Next" to locate one by one all your objects.

Page metrics: first thing to adjust!

A most important but rather underestimated setting, hidden among "advanced" options, supposedly not that worthy of notice! It is not advanced, it is elementary, unavoidable, first thing to check, if you care about the layout of your document. Deciding the layout you need to setup page size, margins, font sizes, etc., and all of these give a result that is going to change a little by the particular printer you choose! Now, you wouldn't like to configure everything carefully only to be ruined by the printer, would you?

The exact same settings may give a slightly[7] different layout because of a particular printer's way to interpret them in the formation of a page. Therefore, you have to invite your printer to the game from the very start!

First go to Word's A d v a n c e d options, in the "Compatibility" section,[8] and activate the option to let Word *use printer metrics to lay out your document*. Then, in Word's P r i n t Setup select the printer you are going to use to print your book, and you are done! Now you see

---

[7] *Slight* doesn't mean *insignificant*. A difference of just 5–10 mm can put some images over your text and increase or decrease the number of your pages!

[8] If Compatibility options are not activated for your document, press Alt+F11 to open the VB Editor, then inside the editor press Ctrl+G to open the Immediate window. Type there the command (without quotes) "ActiveDocument.SetCompatibilityMode 14", press Enter and close the VB Editor to return to your document.

on screen your book as it will be printed, excepting of course quality, since that depends on the resolution of your graphics and the quality of your printer, your paper, even your ink.

If you are going to print in your own printer, to give a copy to your professor or anyone, you can just select this printer in Word's settings — but you can also choose to print first as PDF.

PDF is what you should prefer when you cooperate with a professional publisher. A PDF copy works best for most publishing houses, assuming they even accept other formats, since this way they avoid compatibility problems and stay close to the original layout of a book. Metrics won't change in a PDF document.

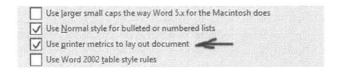

Word supports natively PDF conversions, as you know, but if you have the chance try also a specialized app such as Adobe Acrobat, or even free PDF printers, among which you'll find some quite powerful (check for reviews at www.TheFreeWindows.com).

Just make sure you select in Word's Print settings the exact printer you are going to use for direct printing or for the PDF version of your document. This is your first task, if you work on a document that sooner or later will be printed.

Paper size

Define in Word any paper supported by your printer, but if you plan to use a professional publisher such as Amazon's CreateSpace, you have to consider, even giving priority, to sizes recommended by your publisher.

Choose paper from the start: the layout of your document depends on that, and you avoid unnecessary and annoying work if you are aware of your needs and choose the right size.

6" x 9" (15.24 x 22.86 cm) trim size is popular in bookstores and libraries, which is the reason why many publishers recommend it. You can define it yourself as a custom size in Word's Page Setup panel. To open the full Page Setup panel, just click this small arrow at the corner of the ribbon's Layout > Page Setup section.

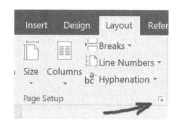

Note that, if you are going to use a regular laser or inkjet printer in home or at work, with paper available in most PC or similar stores, this 6" x 9" paper size is not supported; then you have to resort to "scaled" printing whenever you print a proof locally before you send an official digital copy to your publisher.

WRITING A BOOK OR THESIS IN MICROSOFT WORD

Black & White Books - Industry Standard Trim-Sizes

5" x 8" (12.7 x 20.32 cm)
5.06" x 7.81" (12.9 x 19.8 cm)
5.25" x 8" (13.335 x 20.32 cm)
5.5" x 8.5" (13.97 x 21.59 cm)
6" x 9" (15.24 x 22.86 cm)
6.14" x 9.21" (15.6 x 23.4 cm)
6.69" x 9.61" (17 x 24.4 cm)
7" x 10" (17.78 x 25.4 cm)
7.44" x 9.69" (18.9 x 24.6 cm)
7.5" x 9.25" (19.1 x 23.5 cm)
8" x 10" (20.32 x 25.4 cm)
8.5" x 11" (21.59 x 27.94 cm)

Full-Color Books - Industry Standard Trim-Sizes

5.5" x 8.5" (13.97 x 21.59 cm)
6" x 9" (15.24 x 22.86 cm)
6.14" x 9.21" (15.6 x 23.4 cm)
7" x 10" (17.78 x 25.4 cm)
8" x 10" (20.32 x 25.4 cm)
8.5" x 8.5" (21.59 x 21.59 cm)
8.5" x 11" (21.59 x 27.94 cm)

Custom Trim Sizes

8.25" x 6" (20.955 x 15.24 cm)
8.25" x 8.25" (20.955 x 20.955 cm)
8.5" x 8.5" (21.59 x 21.59 cm)

Modifying the setup of your pages you need to make sure your changes are applied to the w h o l e   d o c u m e n t, unless of course you really want them for a section only.

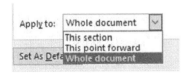

Word's default option in the Page Setup panel, is *This section*. It's at the bottom, and it may pass unnoticed!

In most cases you don't need this limitation. For instance, if you change the size of your margins, forgetting to choose the *Whole document* option in the Drop Down menu, you create a mess in the layout of your pages and you prepare for yourself additional trouble when the time comes to print.

Page margins

As you know, proper margins make a book more enjoyable, even just readable! The exact size of them, beyond a technically necessary length, depends on your taste and on the nature of your work.

> Don't be afraid of margins, but also make sure they work, you don't need your readers to have a sense of wasted space!

Adding more pages to your book, you have to increase *interior* margins, since even more space will be allocated to binding. When you use *glued* binding, that is. Your publisher lets you know the necessary (minimum) size for your margins.

Here is what CreateSpace suggests:

Page Count	Inside Margin	Outside Margins
24 to 150 pages	0.375" (9.53 mm)	at least 0.25" (6.35 mm)
151 to 300 pages	0.5" (12.7 mm)	at least 0.25" (6.35 mm)
301 to 500 pages	0.625" (15.88 mm)	at least 0.25" (6.35 mm)
501 to 700 pages	0.75" (19.05 mm)	at least 0.25" (6.35 mm)
700 to 828 pages	0.875" (22.23 mm)	at least 0.25" (6.35 mm)

Beyond this required size, to adjust your margins optimally try to figure out how much free space your text, headings and graphics need in order to let your readers breath and enjoy.

Things become here highly subjective, but I testify in favor of the following rule as a safe starting point:

Poems and guides like white space, dissertations[9] hate it!

Even if your book contains images that need to bleed to the edges, your text areas should always be limited by some margins.

[9] That is, the final, public, version. While you cooperate with a professor you may need to give copies of (the progress of) your dissertation in double line height, etc.

The Word Ribbon

Word toolbars or ribbons cannot be customized that easily; you have to remove groups of commands, if you don't need them, or create custom groups, in case that you find Word's default configuration inconvenient.

Since default groups are well configured, try first to put them in an order of importance, placing at the left what you use most and moving what you use less to the right part of each ribbon.

As you may have noticed, when you use Word in a small window, some groups are not visible. If you enlarge Word's window, new groups start to appear. You really want to place less useful groups at the right.

Favorite commands or macros can be associated with little icons in Word's title bar for Quick Access, thus immediately acquiring also a keyboard shortcut (Alt + their number in the toolbar), but a most useful tool is Word's Command Search (the "Tell me what you want to do..." search box at the right side, just before your user name), where you start typing the name of any command or function, and the program finds it for you, so that you won't have to look for it in the numerous toolbar icons and menus, where it may not even be included!

For example, where is the *Go to Next Footnote* command? Just start typing "footnote" in Command Search...

Let your style shine!

Aesthetics is not something you can ignore without real cost: it facilitates comprehension, and it supports the pleasure of reading.

As a general rule (exceptions are possible) avoid bold letters and give emphasis with *italics* or e x p a n d e d letters; don't use extremely large or small fonts for normal text, and avoid exaggeration also with line height. Don't use more than one font family, unless it is necessary and somehow usual in your field. Text effects (shadow, reflection, etc.) can be used in elementary school exercises…

Configure basic elements of your style such as paragraph formatting, font sizes and type, just when you start a new document; keep on making adjustments as you proceed with writing, thus realizing what works best for you, for your topic and for your readers. By the time you let it be published, you will be as sure as you can about your book's style.

Contents of this section

The Normal style and template	37
How to find and modify your custom templates	41
How to create new styles	43
How to change easily any manual formatting applied here and there	45
How to export basic Word customizations	46
Resetting the Normal template without losing your customizations	47
Chapters, Sections, Headings	49
Creating Section Breaks	50
Start main chapters on o d d pages	51
Setup different headers and footers for odd and even pages	53
Let your chapters have their own distinct headers	53
Building a u t o m a t i c a l l y individual headers for your chapters	56
How to interrupt a global header	58
How to create global and unique headers in the same document	59
Odd and even headers can follow different styles	60
How to increase or decrease the distance between header (or footer) and body text	61
How to eliminate unnecessary blank space above headings	62
How to p r e s e r v e extra space above your headings	63
Prevent unnecessary horizontal lines	64
Eliminate unnecessary blank space between words when you paste	65
Page numbering can start and stop in any page	65
Page numbers at the corners	67
How to add in your text special paragraphs of n u m b e r e d l i n e s	68
Changing the case of selected text automatically and rapidly	70
Hyphenation	71
Prevent orphan l e t t e r s	72
Prevent orphan w o r d s	73

The Normal style and template

Perhaps you know how important working with styles is, but let me remind here, just in case, this rule:

N e v e r do manually what you can do by applying a style.

Don't just press two times the Enter key to add a blank line as if your PC were an old typewriter. Don't use the Tab key to increase the indent of the first line — avoid a way that seems fast and convenient at the moment but may cause a lot of trouble later on, when you decide perhaps that your distances should be different…

Styles influence a lot of functions in a document, but they are not omnipotent. However, even when a style cannot help, you may not always have to do things manually. A great example is hyphenation.

Hyphenation is important, especially in languages with a lot of long words, such as German or Greek, but also in English. You may have defined in Word the strongest possible hyphenation zone, yet without achieving ideal results: some words that could be broken remain intact, leaving a rather large amount of blank space in the previous line. Do not just press the Minus key to add a hyphen: such hyphens remain even when you change your text and they are not needed anymore. Add an *auto hyphen* by pressing Ctrl+Minus. This hyphen disappears automatically when there is no need for a word to be hyphenated. Pressing Ctrl+Shift+Minus inserts a non-breaking hyphen, i.e. a hyphen that will keep both parts in the same line. This hyphen doesn't regard the layout of a page but the meaning of a word (as in *self-organized, self-made*, etc.), and it won't disappear unless you delete it.[10]

If you have assigned hyphen shortcuts to other tasks in Word or globally, you need to reconfigure them. Go to Insert > Symbol > More > *Special Characters* and customize their shortcuts. While you are there you may like to check and customize the keyboard shortcuts for inserting other common symbols, such as the ©opyright or §ection marks.

Would you prefer this part of your text to start on a new page? *Do not press several times the Enter key* until you start a new page! Ctrl+Enter starts a new page. Even if you modify all your book later, this top-of-the-page paragraph stays at the top, it won't brake the rule.

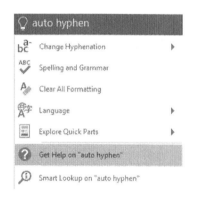

Word provides a nice help system that lets you know what you can do, if you just ask! In Command Search you find also a help section. Just try to keep always in mind this great rule that doesn't seem to be emphasized or even mentioned in Word's help system: avoid doing manually what can be achieved automatically, unless you are absolutely certain you won't face problems later.

---

[10] Note also this difference between hyphens and m— or n– dashes. Usually mdashes separate meanings, while ndashes indicate ranges such as 5–7. "m" stands for "double n", meaning that mdash is double the size of ndash.

In places where you apply manual formatting, you have to return again whenever you want to make changes.

When a *Search and Replace* operation is feasible, your problem can be solved sometimes easily, sometimes with difficulties or even a risk; yet if you avoid manual formatting in favor of using a style, you modify your style and all of its instances change at once anywhere.

Your Normal style is the foundation of the appearance of any document you create. It determines your basic font family and size, paragraph alignment, tab spacing, line and letter spacing…, everything on which even more styles are based and can be created, such as those for your headings, quotations, indexes, etc.

Word comes with a default Normal style you are free to customize, but you have also a way to intervene on a far more significant scale: the Normal t e m p l a t e.

This template is used whenever you start Word, and it includes default styles, the default Normal style, and all those settings that determine the basic look and functionality of a document.

Any changes you make to this template become the default settings for each and every document you will be creating in the future.[11] You can always customize particular documents, but also always having as your starting point your Normal template.

---

[11] You will find the address of the folder that holds your templates, at Word's Options > Advanced > File Locations. Copy this address, then on Word's File menu click O p e n to navigate to the folder of your templates.

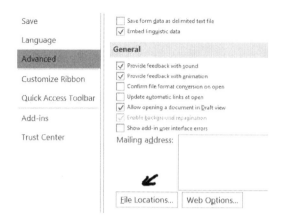

Open in Word the Normal template as if it were a usual document, to modify fonts, margins, spacing, or any elements and settings you'd like. You can use the same commands and features that you use when you customize a document, but remember: any changes you make to this template are meant to form a basic layout for all your future documents.

If your customized Normal template is renamed, damaged, or moved, next time you start Word the program automatically creates a new version, which uses Word's original settings as default: this new version will not include any of the customizations you made to the version that was damaged or deleted.

Always backup any template after you customize it.

Your *Auto Correct* entries, in case you changed anything, are also saved in your Normal template. To export only your *macros*, if you need to give them to a friend or just have a special backup, you can use *.bas* files, a type used by the Visual Basic Editor.

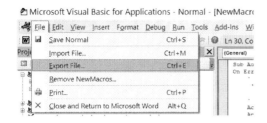

To import one or more macros from a .bas file, when you are in Word use the shortcut Alt+F11 to open the Visual Basic Editor. In the editor go to File > Import, or just press Ctrl+M. In the dialog that opens, find and select the .bas file to import your macros.

To export your macros, open the VB Editor and go to File > Export, or press Ctrl+E.

How to find and modify your custom templates

All your custom templates you may have created for earlier versions of Office are still there; Office doesn't show them by default, yet it's easy to have them available in your Personal tab.

Write the following address in Cortana, or in the "Run" dialogue (Ctrl+R), and press Enter:

%appdata%\Microsoft\Templates\

This opens Windows Explorer in the address of your templates. Copy this address by right-clicking in Explorer's address bar. Then in Word go to File > Options > Save, and paste the address into the *Default personal templates* location box.

[Word Options dialog screenshot showing Save settings with Default local file location and Default personal templates location fields highlighted]

After you have updated the location of your templates, any new templates will be saved there.[12]

To edit a custom template, go to File > Open, and *double click* "This PC".

Browse to *Custom Office Templates* in My Documents or anywhere you save your custom templates.

Click your template and open it.

Make any changes you want, save and close it.

---

[12] In case you had a different folder in the past for your custom templates, you can just use that address.

How to create new styles

Word provides a lot of convenient templates you can use as they are or modify. However, if you follow, as you should, this precious rule, to never do manually what can be done with a style, sooner or later the time comes for you to create new styles.

Go to the Styles pane at the ribbon, and press this little arrow:

Then select the option to *Create a Style*

Give your style a name that helps you to recall easily its purpose.

For instance, if you want it to double the space between the lines of a paragraph, you can name it Double Line Height.

Style type lets you specialize. In most cases you need the option of *paragraph and character*.

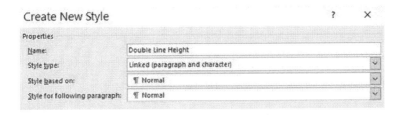

The next option (*Based on*) lets you inherit the settings from already existing styles.

The final one (*Following paragraph*) lets you define what style Word uses when you press Enter to add a new paragraph.

If your style will be used occasionally for a single paragraph, you should choose as style of the *Following paragraph* the Normal style.

Several scenarios are possible in creating new styles, with Word being here flexible, clear and convenient.

Think carefully and make some tests until you are satisfied with what you see, but you can always easily modify your styles to fine tune, or even make full scale changes.

A benefit of doing this when you *start* working on a project, is that *you are going to live with your styles* as you write, realizing naturally what works best, what may become boring in the course of time, etc.

Until you finish your book you will have achieved an appearance that satisfies both your taste and the needs of your content, hopefully the needs of your readers too.

Word provides a preview of all fonts that are installed in the OS and are available to be used in a document, but you may like to try also free specialized applications that will form categories of fonts to present them on a list featuring text, sizes and styles you are invited to customize; they even let you browse and test fonts not installed on Windows, from any folder you like, being also able to directly install or uninstall system fonts, etc. You will find reviews for free font viewers and managers at www.TheFreeWindows.com

How to change easily any manual formatting applied here and there

If you are lazy and neglect the use of styles, don't be surprised when you face this problem in your document. In some sentences, paragraphs or even pages and chapters, you applied manually formatting changes you need now to revert or modify, while you don't even remember all those places that were customized!

Modifying the Normal or any style won't help; manually customized elements won't obey to style changes, unless they are selected one by one and modified.

To solve this problem, first of all make sure you have all of Word's commands visible at the toolbar: you may need to maximize your window to see everything.

Locate in your document and select just a small part of a single element that contains this custom formatting you need to modify.

Then go to Home > Editing (usually at the far right side of the ribbon), press the Select button and choose the option, *Select Text with Similar Formatting*. You can find this command also by using the Command Search.

Locate the Normal style,[13] and click on it to bring all of this selected elements back to the Normal style. Of course you can apply any style you like, perhaps a new one that is not identical with the Normal, this way changing all instances of manual formatting to a style you can later modify to apply instantly global changes.

How to export basic Word customizations

If you need to transfer basic customizations of yours, such as default font family and size, your macros, etc., to your laptop or elsewhere, this can be achieved by replacing Word's *default* normal t e m - p l a t e with the one containing your customizations.

To locate your customized normal template go to Word's Options > Advanced > General > F i l e   L o c a t i o n s.

Open the File Locations panel to find the *User Templates* location. Open your templates folder, right click your Normal template to copy and paste it in the relevant folder of any other Office installation you are using, or just in your backup folder to transfer it later wherever you need.

Always backup templates you replace.

---

[13] At the *Styles* section of the *Home* ribbon.

Resetting the Normal template without losing your customizations

When you believe there is something wrong with your normal template, and your customizations are not the cause of this problem, you may like to reset the normal template, bring it back to the original Word settings, but without losing your styles, macros, custom auto correct entries, etc.

Here is what you can do. First, find the location of your normal template as was described above. Then close Word and rename your normal template to any name you like. Open again Word: a new normal template is created by Word automatically. Now,

1) Copy your styles: Locate your old, renamed, normal template in Windows Explorer and open it in Word. Go to Developer > View Macros > *Organizer*, and copy all or any styles from the old normal template to the new.

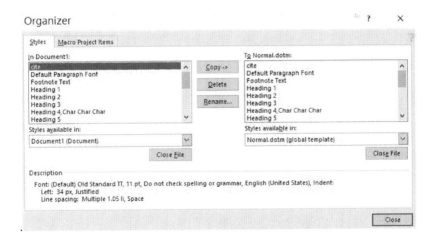

2) Copy your macros: Follow the same steps for your macros. Open the Macro Project Items tab in the Organizer. In the left pane you see the macros that are included in your old normal template. In the right pane select (if it isn't already active) your current (new) normal template. Copy your macro projects from the old to your new normal template.

3) Export your Ribbons and Quick Access Toolbar: Go to Options > Customize Ribbon > *Import / Export*, to save or restore your Ribbon customizations. This includes the Quick Access Toolbar settings. When you import your custom configuration from your older template, any pre-existing customizations in your new normal template are lost. Always create an export of your current settings before importing a Ribbon file, in case you change your mind later and need to revert these changes.

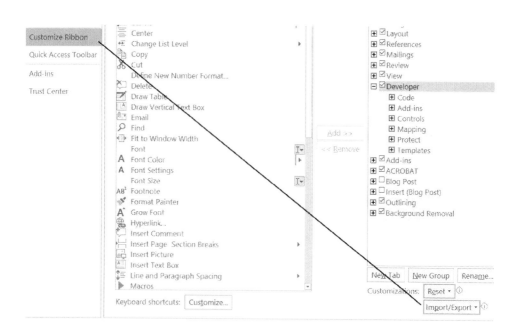

Chapters, Sections, Headings

First thing you need to understand when you create a book with chapters, is the *technical* aspect of sections.

Sections let you create your chapters as you want them to avoid unnecessary, annoying and sometimes risky editing.

A section can contain several parts of a document, with chapters or not, but always start a new section for e a c h of your chapters. This way you can customize your chapters, perhaps to place unique content in their headers, such as their t i t l e s.

Even if you prefer to have the book title in all of your headers, still start a new section for each chapter, even if only to have a b l a n k header in the first page of a chapter, and let its title be gloriously alone at the top of your body text!

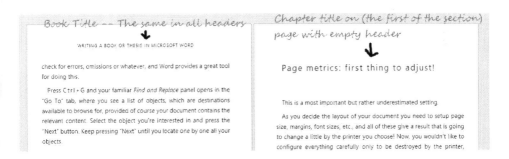

Creating Section Breaks

Start a new section whenever you apply a heading style.

To do that even with the keyboard, you can press Alt+P (this activates the Layout tab of the ribbon), then B (to activate the Breaks menu), and finally a letter such as D, to insert an Odd Page Break, or N to insert a Next Page Break, etc.

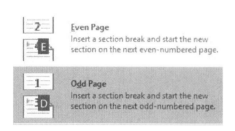

For our convenience Word explains the function of each break already in the menu. As you can guess, after a while, if you don't neglect the use of sections, you won't need to read this information.

Keep in mind an important difference:

Page breaks regard 'small scale' settings, when you need for a paragraph to start always at the top of a page (page break) or column (column break), or when you need for a picture caption to be always clearly separated from body text (text wrapping break), without, in all of these cases, planning any other layout change.

Section breaks regard 'large scale' differences.

For instance, inserting a "new page" *section* break, you start a new page, as in page break, but also a page that belongs to a new layout 'zone' of your document, where you can have different margins than the rest of your document, different headers and footers, even different page size, etc.

Let's see a few critical settings that are not obvious, while they influence the structure of a chapter in a way most authors would like to know.

Start main chapters on odd pages

Main chapters need to face the reader directly, they need to be on odd pages. If some of them are not associated with an odd section break, don't be disappointed, Word macros can help.

The following macro inserts an odd page break before any style you'd like, assuming of course that some heading style is applied on chapter titles.

This macro inserts an odd page break before the "Heading 2" style; you may change this with any style used in your own document. (To avoid writing this macro in the Visual Basic Editor, just import it in Word from www.TheFreeWindows.com)

```
Sub InsertOddPageSectionBreak()
Dim rngDcm As Range
Dim rngTmp As Range
Set rngDcm = ActiveDocument.Range
With rngDcm.Find
.Style = "Heading 2"
While .Execute
rngDcm.Select
Set rngTmp = rngDcm.Duplicate
rngTmp.Collapse
rngTmp.Select
If Asc(rngTmp.Characters.First.Previous) <> 12 And _
Asc(rngTmp.Characters.First) <> 12 Then
```

```
rngTmp.InsertBreak Type:=wdSectionBreakOddPage
End If
rngDcm.Collapse Direction:=wdCollapseEnd
Wend
End With
End Sub
```

If your document uses section breaks for chapters, but breaks that won't start on odd pages, open the *Page Setup* panel > Layout, and change the top option to "Odd page", applying this change to "whole document". If you need to change a specific chapter only, place the cursor in this chapter, skip the "whole document" option and select odd page for "this section" only.[14]

---

[14] To remove an unwanted page break without damaging the layout of your document, sometimes you need to view and delete directly its code by typing Ctrl+Shift+*

Setup different headers and footers for odd and even pages

What if you wanted a different header for odd and even pages, a rather common feature, to have, for instance, your book's title in all the even headers, and chapter titles in the headers of odd pages, or to have page numbers at the outer corners of your headers or footers?

To do this, open the *Page Setup* panel and go to Layout. At the "Headers and footers" section check the option to have different odd and even headers and footers.

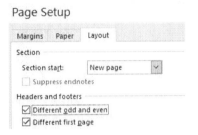

Let your chapters have their own distinct headers

Did you find suddenly that changing a header of a chapter changes the headers of all your chapters — although you had the caution to create several sections?

It's not enough to create a section for a chapter, you need to make sure that a section won't inherit the header or footer content of the previous section. Unfortunately, the way to achieve this separation is not obvious and it might seem a little complicated before you become familiar enough with layout settings in Word.

Here is what you need to do whenever you create a new section, wanting for it to have its own unique headers.

Double click anywhere at the upper limit of your document, the header area. Word now changes focus and lets you edit your header text instead of body text.

Is this a distinct or a "shared" header? If you edit this one, will you modify also the headers of the previous or even of the next chapter?

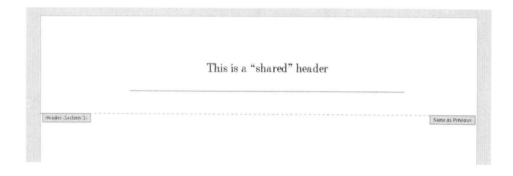

Notice that little box at the bottom right corner; it warns that this header is and will remain "Same as Previous".

When you edit this header, your changes are applied also to the header of the previous section, in order for the headers of both sections to remain "the same".

If your next chapter's header is also "Same as Previous", then changing this one you change both the next and the previous chapter's header!

In Word's toolbar > Design > Navigation, find the "Link to Previous" option. If selected, Word gives it a shade that differs from the normal ribbon background.

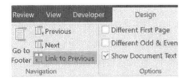

Clicking to deactivate it you remove the current section's header link to the previous section. This means, editing the header of the current section won't change the header of the previous — and the opposite: whenever you change the previous section's header, this one remains the same.

If you prefer also that your edits won't influence the next chapter's header, you must unlink that too by editing its own header to deactivate the "Link to Previous" option.

Note that, when you work on a small Word window, the Design tab may not be visible; you may not even remember which tab holds the command to unlink headers!

Just double click the header area to enable editing of your header, and then go to the familiar Command Search box. Start to write the word "link" until Word finds the "Link to Previous" option which you can click immediately to deactivate it and separate the current section's headers from the headers of the preceding section. Just make sure you have already activated editing in the header area, before you enter the Command Search box.

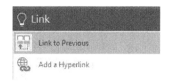

You know the two sections' headers are unlinked because the *Same as Previous* box at the bottom right corner disappears. Don't forget that if you want a *discontinuation* of headers, i.e. your next chapter to keep being as it was and not follow the header you are currently editing, you need to unlink the header of that section too, before you edit the header of the current section.

Building automatically individual headers for your chapters

You can follow the steps described above to let your chapters have unique headers, however, there is also a way, in certain cases, to avoid the "unlink" routine completely, without sacrificing your custom headers!

Word automation or field codes let you insert anywhere in your document several data that can be updated automatically, such as tables of contents.

You can find a list of fields easily by going to Header and Footer Tools > Document Info > Field, or by writing in Command Search the words *Add document info*, then going to Field.

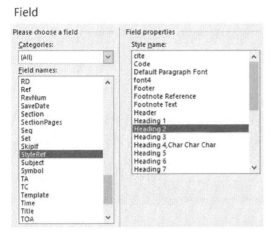

In the dialogue that opens go to Field names > *StyleRef*, click on it and in the right pane double click the heading that agrees with your chapters' titles. If you have titles of multiple levels (Heading 1, 2, etc.) select the heading level(s) of the titles you'd like to appear in your headers.

This inserts in the headers a code representing the current section's heading, which is your chapter title. Now whenever a new heading of this type (1, 2, or whatever you selected) appears in your document, this particular chapter's title shows up automatically in the headers of your book and remains until a new chapter begins.

You may add normal text besides field codes, but this text remains the same in all headers of all chapters. Let's say you have a header in the form: *Chapter + FieldCode*. The word "Chapter" remains the same throughout.

To have unique words or phrases that won't be generated by a field code, you need the manual separation (unlinking) of neighboring sections' headers and footers.

How to interrupt a global header

To interrupt a global header, go to the first page of the section after the section that should not have this header, enter the header pane by double clicking at the top side of the page, go to *Header and Footer Tools* at the ribbon, and press the Link to Previous button to remove the link.

The button is deactivated and this header won't follow anymore what is written in the header of the previous section.

Then go to the section you want to customize; unlink this too from its previous, and now it's safe to edit your header without changing anything in other sections' headers.

> Repeat the same steps three times, for the first, the second (even) and the third (odd) page of all sections you unlink, in case you configured (at the *Page Setup* of your document) your sections to have *different odd and even headers and footers* and *different first page*.

If more sections in your document need a new singular header, follow the same routine, unlink their headers from the previous and next section's headers.[15]

---

[15] Since a header inherits all content from the previous section's header, if you want to interrupt this continuation in several parts of your document, start from the very last, change the last section that needs a custom header, then go on to change the preceding section's header that needs to be

How to create global and unique headers in the same document

You may have noticed that sometimes a book uses the left (even) header for the *book* title, which remains the same in all headers, and the right (odd) header for *chapter* titles. You can achieve this easily by selecting in Page Setup the option to have *different odd and even* headers (and footers — you can't have different headers without having also different footers).

In the left header just write the title of your book. In the right header insert the *StyleRef* heading field that will be automatically updated whenever you change chapter, the way we already saw. In both cases *leave your headers interlinked*, otherwise you have to enter this information again whenever a new section starts.

Don't forget, when you have different odd and even headers you need to edit both an even and an odd header of a section, providing different content for each of them, if you want them distinct, or the same content, if you want them identical, unless for a particular section you uncheck in Page Setup the option of having different odd and even headers.

---

changed, etc. This helps to avoid mistakes and unnecessary editing, since sometimes we unlink the current section from its previous, but we forget to unlink also the next section from the current, this way applying without knowing it our edits to each and every section after the current.

Insert a Section break whenever you start a new chapter, to enjoy more control over your chapters. Different sections can have different margins, different page numbering, different odd and even headers, even different paper.

Odd and even headers can follow different styles

While it's easy to have different content in your headers or footers for odd and even pages, you may face this seemingly strange behavior. Changing, for instance, the alignment of an odd header, your even headers change too, although in Page Setup you activated the option for "different odd and even" headers and footers!

The Page Setup difference regards content, not style. Your problem is introduced by the style that you use in your header or footer, which is applied to all headers. Normally this style is called "header" (or "footer").

In the first card that appears when you click to Modify your style, make sure that the option *Automatically update* is unchecked.

Automatic update means that any change you make in a header is passed to the style, and thus it is applied universally, to odd and even headers alike!

When you clear this option headers keep all features defined already in the style, but any changes you make *manually* in a particular header from that moment on are applied only to interlinked headers, odd or even.

To make things even better you can create a new *style* for the header or footer you need to differentiate, especially when you are going to play a lot with the format of your headers or footers.

How to increase or decrease the distance between header (or footer) and body text

Now, you have this great header in your document, but it's so close to body text, you wish there was more space in between!

No obvious way to do that (as so many things in Word!), not even if you resort to the ruler.[16]

Open the *Page Setup* dialogue and go to the Layout tab, where you see your header settings referring to the distance of a header from the paper's top edge.

Your header is going to keep this distance from the edge, whatever the size of your margin might be.

---

[16] Which you shouldn't do anyway — remember? Try to use global settings such as styles, that you can modify to achieve easily global effects.

If you set your header 2 cm away from the edge, and your margin as tall as 1 cm, then your margin will actually be 2 cm, since Word adds automatically the space required to avoid putting your body text at the top of your header!

Therefore, to increase the distance between header and body text, first decide where your header should be, then increase your margin until it passes your header as much as you need: your header remains unmovable to its predefined distance, while extra margin height is added below, pushing body text away from the header.

In the previous example, if I wanted the main text to have a 5 cm distance from the header, I should set my margin to 7 cm, adding 5 cm to the 2 cm distance of the header from the edge.

To decrease a large distance between header and body, just decrease your margin, bringing it closer to header height. In a similar way you can increase or decrease the distance between footer and body text.

How to eliminate unnecessary blank space above headings

Let's say your style requires some extra blank space before your heading.

This space is useless when a heading appears with nothing above it. Is there a way you could eliminate automatically this type of blank space?

A manual way would be to change paragraph style when blank space is not needed.

This solution is burdensome, and is also possible only when all editing is finished and you are absolutely sure you won't be changing anything; otherwise your headings may move in the document, needing again this blank space you have manually removed.

An automatic way would be to have your headings start always on a new page. Then blank space is not needed anymore — and is even removed by Word automatically.

How to preserve extra space above your headings

You may have created this great paragraph or heading style that makes things distinct by adding some blank space, only to find that Word doesn't respect your style, eliminating this additional space.

If your heading appears at the top of the page, there is nothing you can do!

Word refuses to add there any "space before", but, if you insist on having it, you can type some invisible text before this paragraph, such as a simple dot in the color of your paper, to make Word believe that additional space is indeed allowed.

Prevent unnecessary horizontal lines

Word enters horizontal lines automatically. If you realize immediately that you don't need one, you can just press Ctrl+Z or the Undo button to remove it.

What if you wrote a couple of pages and you are not willing to sacrifice all your effort just to remove this uninvited line?

This line is a border. To remove it place above it the cursor and go to the "Home" ribbon, in the "Paragraph" tab, where you find border options.

Press the little arrow at the right of the button for border options, and select "No border". You can also type "borders" at Command Search and go to Border Style > No borders!

This way you can get rid of the annoying border, since a simple delete just skips it!

You can also disable completely the auto-line feature by going to Proofing > Auto Correct, and deactivating the option, *Apply as you type* > Border lines.

Eliminate unnecessary blank space between words when you paste

Do you need to paste a word or phrase in several locations at *exact* positions, for instance, just beside some punctuation mark? You may find that Word won't let you do it, always adding a space between this mark and your phrase!

To solve your problem, go to File > Options > Advanced > Cut, Copy and Paste > Smart Cut and Paste > Settings, and clear the option "Adjust sentence and word spacing automatically".

Now you can paste your text exactly where you need it.

Of course, usually you like that Word adds this blank space, you can reactivate the option after you finish your special task.

Page numbering can start and stop in any page

Word lets you insert page numbers easily. You can even have them start from any number you like, or include chapter titles beside numbers. Let's see a case that is useful, even absolutely necessary, yet not that obvious.

What if you wanted to leave some of your pages without page numbers? This is just normal for the first pages of a book.

Go to the page where you want numbering to start. This can be whatever page – the third, fourth, sixteenth…

Insert a Section Break, if there is none.

Unlink this section from the previous: activate Print Layout view, if you have not already, and double click the footer area of this section, if you are going to insert page numbers in the footer of your document, or else open the section's header. Press the Unlink button in the *Header and Footer Tools* ribbon (you can find it with Command Search, if it is not visible).

Go to Insert > Page Number, and pick a Microsoft template. Select some of the first options, *simple numbers without graphics*, if you need to customize your numbering style easily.

Do this also for the footer of the second page of this section if in *Page Setup* you have activated "different first page", and do it once more for the footer of the third page of this section if in Page Setup you have activated "different odd and even pages".

If you don't need page numbering in your previous section, not even with invisible numbers, go to Insert > Page Number > *Format Page Number*, and select the "Start at 1" option.

Let's hope some day Microsoft understands how common such a numbering is, particularly in scholarly publications, and just provide a simple option to "start page numbering from this page", even with relevant sub-options, such as "leave without numbering all pages before the current" or "change numbering format (e.g. use Latin numbers) for all pages before the current", etc.

Page numbers at the corners

Here is how you can let your numbers align to page corners — at the right for odd pages, at the left for even pages (or the opposite, which is not usual).

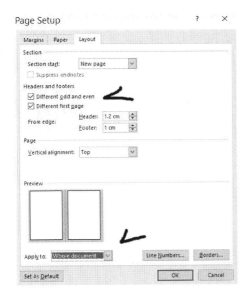

First define the Page Layout of your document as "different for odd and even pages," and as "different first page."

Don't forget to make this adjustment global, that is valid for the "whole document".

Open the footer of an odd page, but n o t of the first page of that section.

Follow this rule, which is rather basic in setting up a book: *leave the first page of each of your main chapters without a page number and without a header.*

Insert page numbering to odd pages and align it to the right or left.

The normal placement for odd page numbers is center or right.

Open the footer of an even page — again, not the first page of that section — insert page numbering and align the number as you wish, normally at the center or at the left corner.

How to add in your text special paragraphs of numbered lines

You may need some parts of your text in numbered lines. Here is an example. The text is from Beowulf.

> *Lo! the Spear-Danes' glory through splendid achievements*
> *The folk-kings' former fame we have heard of,*
> 3 *How princes displayed then their prowess-in-battle.*
> *Oft Scyld the Scefing from scathers in numbers*
> *From many a people their mead-benches tore.*
> 6 *Since first he found him friendless and wretched,*
> *The earl had had terror: comfort he got for it,*
> *Waxed 'neath the welkin, world-honor gained,*
> 9 *Till all his neighbors o'er sea were compelled to*
> *Bow to his bidding and bring him their tribute:*
> *An excellent atheling! After was borne him*
> 12 *A son and heir, young in his dwelling,*
> *Whom God-Father sent to solace the people.*

It needs some effort to create a paragraph like this, with numbered lines, unnumbered text on the same page immediately before and after, featuring a lot of white space at the side of numbers, even different size and typeface for numbered text and numbers.

In the panel that lets you number your text (*Layout > Line Numbers*) you can define the distance between numbers and text, but there is no option to apply numbering to *selected* text only, or to *current paragraph*, or even just to *current page*. Word applies line numbering only to sections. Therefore, any text, parts of a text, a paragraph, whatever you need numbered, has to be the only content of a distinct section. For the paragraph above I used a Continuous section break, that would let me place regular, unnumbered, text immediately before and after numbered lines.

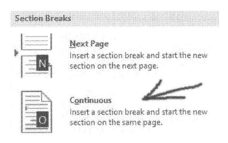

Then in Page Setup I modified this section to have a larger margin, in order for line numbers to enjoy more blank space at their side; Word by default places line numbers inside the margin where they won't even be printed!

Word's default format of line numbering follows the default paragraph style. To change this, open the Styles sidebar (*Home > Styles*) and locate the Line Number style.[17]

Right-click the Line Number style to modify it. You can have numbers of whatever font size and family.

---

[17] You need to enable first the view of all styles, not only "used", etc.

Changing the case of selected text automatically and rapidly

You may not know or forget this keyboard shortcut that lets you immediately change the case of selected text in a Word document, if everything is in capital letters and you want it in small or in title case letters, etc.

The change of case is most useful if you paste in Word texts from sources formatted in a different style.

It may also be useful for your own text if in the future your stylistic preferences change.

Press Shift+F3 and keep on pressing it until you find the case that you need.

Shift+F3 lets you cycle through ALL CAPS, all lowercase, and All Title Case.

If you need even more options, just go to Home > Font, and click the Change Case button.

Sentence case.
lowercase
UPPERCASE
Capitalize Each Word
tOGGLE cASE

ALL CAPS is like shouting, be careful when to use it, perhaps in some headings or the header, in a small font size.

Hyphenation

You can easily configure Word to hyphenate your document, but there is a detail you may not know. For hyphenation to work you need Spelling and Grammar Check enabled, even if you hide the errors to avoid distraction.

When hyphenation won't work, although in Word's Options Spelling is enabled, go to the style you need hyphenated, usually the "Normal" style, and modify it.

In its "Language" section un-check the option *Do not check spelling or grammar*.

Press OK and you see immediately your text hyphenated!

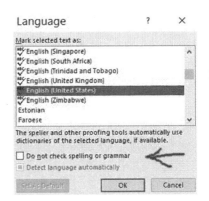

Prevent orphan letters

Used independently of any style, this option influences a single word and nothing else: if you select a word and disable Spelling for this particular (instance of a) word, it won't be hyphenated.

This can prove very useful, when you find that hyphenation leaves a single letter on a different line!

I even created an icon in my Quick Access toolbar to easily deactivate Grammar and Spell Check, thus disabling hyphenation for particular words. My hyphenation zone is the strongest that Word allows, but this may cause the orphan letters problem.

To find this option use Command Search. Write "language" and go to "Set Proofing Language". Then disable Spelling and Grammar Check. Your choice influences only this instance of the selected word; Grammar and Spelling Check remains active for the rest of your document as before.

Prevent orphan words

This is not a hyphenation problem, save in a broad sense, regarding the amount of words not in a line, but in a page.

It's a common and great problem in Word, that a few words can be left isolated in the previous or the next page. You wouldn't expect in a professional publication blank pages with nothing but a few words or a line, the ending of the previous page's paragraph, or even pages ending with a few words from the start of the next page's paragraph.

To avoid this mess, modify your Normal style's Paragraph settings.

Go to "Line and page breaks" and select the option "Widow / Orphan control."

Word is not always able to avoid orphans, even after you activate this option.

You can also use these even stronger options, to "keep lines together", all the lines of a paragraph, or "keep with next", but then you may find that a very large amount of useless blank space is created.

When these solutions won't work, you have to resort to manual adjustments. In the problematic page, or even in the whole section, try to decrease or increase line height, letter spacing, paragraph spacing, etc., as much as you see that the difference from the rest of your text is insignificant and can remain unnoticed.

You may also like to become more laconic and remove content, a number of words or sentences that you don't really need, use fewer examples, remove a less needed graphic, anything that would make this page shorter, without betraying the quality of your work.

In case that your page should become a little longer, make it even more informative, add an example, present more evidence, etc.

Be powerful

Being powerful doesn't mean to use all those tools Microsoft Word provides: it means knowing both what your text needs and how Word can support your work.

In a thesis you are going to have footnotes, a bibliography, one or more indexes, one or more tables of contents; in a novel most probably you won't need footnotes, not even a table of contents…

Contents of this section

How to import your WordPress posts	77
Importing several Word documents into your main document	77
How to split your pages vertically to put side by side two texts	78
Footnote issues	80
Open by default a larger footnotes pane in Draft view	80
Let there be columns in Footnotes!	82
Creating a Table of Contents	83
How to create multiple tables of contents in the same document	84
Toggle Field Codes View without losing focus of your current position	86
A bibliography with style	89
Creating Indexes of persons or topics	91
Index Subentries	91
Cross-references	92
Time to build your Index!	93
How to create more than one Index in the same document	94
If your Index ignores your custom font style	98
Adding Pictures	100

| How to protect image quality | 100 |
| Cropping your images | 101 |

Inserting Excel Objects 105

How to import your WordPress posts

A couple of blog posts can be easily incorporated in a document in the usual copy–paste way, but what if you need hundreds of them? Freeware such as *WordPress2Doc*[18] may convert blog posts as included in WordPress XML exports. First export your posts at the WordPress backend. Then convert all of them to Word documents, and delete what you don't need, since conversion is really fast. The following chapter lets you know how to import to your main document a number of other documents, whether they come from a WordPress export or not.

Importing several Word documents into your main document

To import in your main document your converted WordPress posts or any other document, go to Insert > Object > *Text from file*. Select all the documents that you want to incorporate, and import them in your main document.

As with all commands, you can find the *Insert Object* option with Command Search, if it's not visible or if you prefer to avoid looking for it in Word's toolbars.

---

[18] Check www.TheFreeWindows.com for downloads.

How to split your pages vertically to put side by side two texts

Word does not provide this kind of layout, considering it a task for desktop publishing applications, such as Microsoft Publisher or Adobe InDesign. There is a simple workaround, yet not without limitations.

You won't be able to use two *pages*, an even and an odd, as a single space that can be 'split' in facing parts, for the original text and for a translation. You can have somehow facing *columns* on single pages, but not facing *pages*.

To split just one or even a series of single pages, create a table with two cells, in Table Properties > Table > Options adjust cell spacing to be enough for a clear distinction of content, and write or paste each text to its own cell.

If your texts are several pages long, create more cells, dividing the whole work in parts even if it's not already divided, to keep it well synchronized and also to protect it from a possible inability of Word to handle a huge table in just a couple of cells.

You don't need a cell for each and every page, just enter one whenever you need to synchronize your text, when a side of it tends to be much longer than the other. For instance, a translation usually surpasses the original.

When you find it convenient, remove all borders from your table, unless you want them also in the printed version, but this would be ugly. You can also remove them the very moment you create your table, letting Word's non-printing *gridlines* guide you.[19]

---

[19] Activate gridlines using the same panel that controls a table's borders. As always, Command Search too can help.

Footnote issues

There is nothing tricky in inserting notes, and perhaps you already have used them in your work. Some functionality may be missing, such as having them follow one another horizontally and not only vertically, but what already exists is great, yet not without annoyances.

Open by default a larger footnotes pane in Draft view

In Draft view, an excellent mode when you need to focus on editing your notes, Word restricts the notes pane to very small dimensions. You have to drag and resize the pane or always scroll to edit long notes. Even if you resize the pane, next time you open it to edit your notes it will be small again, it doesn't remember your preference!

There is no setting that lets you define the default size of the footnotes pane. To make more room try this macro (you can also download it from www.TheFreeWindows.com to import it in Word easily)

```
Sub ViewFtnotesLarge()
Dim nPaneSize As Long
'Change nPaneSize at will
nPaneSize = 42
With ActiveWindow
Select Case .ActivePane.View.Type
Case wdPrintView, wdWebView, wdPrintPreview
If .View.SeekView = wdSeekFootnotes Then
.View.SeekView = wdSeekMainDocument
ElseIf .View.SeekView = wdSeekMainDocument Then
.View.SeekView = wdSeekFootnotes
End If
```

```
Case Else
If .Panes.Count > 1 Then
.Panes(2).Close
Else
.View.SplitSpecial = wdPaneFootnotes
.SplitVertical = nPaOneSize
Selection.MoveRight Unit:=wdCharacter, Count:=1
ActiveWindow.SmallScroll Down:=12
Selection.MoveRight Unit:=wdCharacter, Count:=1
End If
End Select
End With
End Sub
```

Assign a keyboard shortcut to open your footnote pane with this macro instead of the default Word command. Pane size is expressed by the *nPaneSize* variable. The value of 42 means that 42% of Word's window goes to main text, 58% to the footnotes pane. You can change this ratio at will.

When the footnotes pane opens, the cursor goes to the top left corner and you are able to see as much text as possible. This is not happening if you use a macro to open a larger pane. In this case the cursor goes to the bottom left corner, and you can see just the first line of the footnote you are interested in! All remaining space is wasted displaying previous footnotes! The macro contains the following part to fix precisely this problem. You may like to experiment with number 12 to match the size of your footnotes pane in case you customize the macro.

```
Selection.MoveRight Unit:=wdCharacter, Count:=1
ActiveWindow.SmallScroll Down:=12
Selection.MoveRight Unit:=wdCharacter, Count:=1
```

Let there be columns in Footnotes!

Word is able to format footnotes in columns, even if your body text does not use columns at all.

Or you may have a body text in 2 columns and your footnotes in 4 columns.

Note that this is possible in footnotes only, you cannot have columns in endnotes.

To take advantage of this feature you have to save your document in docx format, as most Word users do anyway.

The docx format may be sometimes a little slower, but it provides increased security and more features such as better editing and higher fidelity of images, features not available in the formerly official doc format.

Creating a Table of Contents

To insert a Table of Contents is as easy as going to Word's Reference tab and selecting a template. You can also design yourself a custom ToC as you like it.

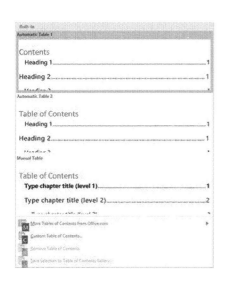

It's not difficult to customize later a built-in type. Entries are created automatically from styles, usually headings, but you can change even this.

Try some default templates for your ToC, before you build a custom table.

Whenever you need to customize the appearance of a Table of Contents, open the Styles pane (Home ribbon) and modify any or all TOC styles that are used in your table.

Where would you like your table to be, at the start or at the end of your book? At the start, a ToC functions also as an overview or as a sort of 'introduction', while at the end it keeps mainly if not only its function to let a reader find easily a particular section.

Both locations are usual, just try to make your entries, i.e. your chapter titles, clear enough, and also apply some formatting differentiations, if your table contains *a lot* of entries. Relevant parts of your ToC can also be offered at the start of main sections, which brings us to the next chapter.

How to create multiple tables of contents in the same document

It sounds complicated, but it's not! If your main Table of Contents contains *a lot* of entries, you may like to add to each of your main sections a smaller table of its own contents to help your readers refresh their memory and gain a better orientation.

First, you need to create a distinct Word bookmark for each of your sections that will host their own ToC.

Go to Outline view, select only headings and hide body text.

Select all headings that belong to your first section for which you'd like a partial ToC, and *Insert a bookmark* (you can find the Insert bookmark command easily with Command Search, as you know).

Give a name that resembles the section's title, making sure it *won't* contain spaces. For instance, if your section is about Market Economies, you can name this bookmark MarketEconomies.

Repeat the same steps for each section that will host its own partial ToC.

Then go to your main ToC and press Alt + F9 (or right click and select the option *Toggle Field Codes*), to let Word show your ToC's *field code* instead of the actual table. Field codes are technical descriptions that Word interprets to form the structure and contents of ToCs. Here is an example:

```
{ TOC \o "1-5" \u }
```

After the field code is revealed, copy and paste it wherever you want your first section's partial ToC to appear, normally at the start of the section. Then add to this code the name of the section's *bookmark* as the value of a new "b" switch. For "Market Economies", the example mentioned above, your code would become:

```
{ TOC \o "1-5" \u b\ MarketEconomies }
```

Press again Alt+F9 (or right click and select the option to *Toggle Field Codes*). Right click inside the ToC and select to update. The partial ToC for this section should appear in all its glory!

If your document contains many Tables of Contents, you don't need to update them one by one before you create a PDF version. Go to Options > Display > Printing options, and let Word *update all fields before printing*. This auto-update includes also your Indexes, any chapter titles inserted automatically in headers, etc.

You can also update all your fields, including Tables of Contents, anytime manually using a keyboard shortcut,[20] after you select the whole document (Ctrl+A).

For each of your ToCs the program asks if you want to update page numbers or rebuild the entire table; answer according to changes you've made. The safest choice,

---

[20] Normally F9 or Alt+Shift+U, which of course you can customize.

especially after a lot of editing, would be to rebuild the entire tables, just in case you've edited some chapter title and forgot it.

To stay on the current page and avoid losing your focus, after a manual update finishes do not use the keyboard, use your mouse to click on the page. This deselects the document and gives focus to the current page.

Toggle Field Codes View without losing focus of your current position

When you work with Field Codes to edit a Table of Contents, you may face this serious issue. *Just by activating Field Codes View* Word loses focus! You may instantly find yourself many pages away from the page you try to edit!

To solve this I use a simple macro that performs three tasks. First, it creates a temporary bookmark in the current location, where I wish to return and restore focus after activation of Field Codes View. I use the name *ToggleFieldCodesBookmark*, but you can change it with whatever you prefer, provided it remains unique, not to be found anywhere in your document.

Then my macro toggles Field Codes View: if normal view is active, the macro activates Field Codes view, and the opposite.

Finally, the macro locates the bookmark created in the first step, and removes it, this way restoring focus where I was before the change of Field Codes View, simultaneously clearing up the workspace. As always, you are welcome to download this macro too from www.TheFreeWindows.com to import it in Word easily.

```
Sub FieldCodesEasyToggle()
Selection.TypeText Text:="ToggleFieldCodesBookmark"
    Selection.Find.ClearFormatting
    Selection.Find.Replacement.ClearFormatting
ActiveWindow.View.ShowFieldCodes = _
 Not ActiveWindow.View.ShowFieldCodes
    With Selection.Find
        .Text = "ToggleFieldCodesBookmark"
        .Replacement.Text = ""
        .Forward = True
        .Wrap = wdFindContinue
        .Format = False
        .MatchCase = False
        .MatchWholeWord = False
        .MatchWildcards = False
        .MatchSoundsLike = False
        .MatchAllWordForms = False
    Selection.Find.Execute
    If Selection = "ToggleFieldCodesBookmark" Then
    Selection.Delete
    End If
    End With
End Sub
```

I tried also an alternative solution that avoids the creation of a bookmark:

```
Sub FieldCodesEasyToggle()
Dim currentPosition As Range
Set currentPosition = Selection.Range
ActiveWindow.View.ShowFieldCodes = _
 Not ActiveWindow.View.ShowFieldCodes
 currentPosition.Select
End Sub
```

Returning to the initial location, this shorter macro won't focus on the top but on the bottom of the page, which means that to continue editing you have to scroll down. I give you also this macro here, since it's very short, in case you'd like to try it and see if you can make it work for you.

Whatever macro you decide to use, just assign it a keyboard shortcut. I use Ctrl+Alt+F9 because it resembles the original Alt+F9 Field Codes View toggle shortcut.

A bibliography with style

It's clear and obvious how to create a bibliography in Word, problems show up with styles.[21] They are not as many as needed, and you cannot customize the existing ones easily, using convenient commands in Word's graphical interface. Inserting a citation too cannot be customized.

Until Word improves on these, I'm afraid we'll have to use separate free or commercial extensions, or even compile our bibliographies manually, at least the citations. For example, I don't want in my footnotes an impersonal / mechanical citation type, such as "Fitzgerald, 1925"; I prefer "F. Scott Fitzgerald, *The Great Gatsby*".

This of course depends not only on personal taste or universal academic requirements but also on the subject of your book. A dissertation in Mathematics may very well use a mechanical style, but in Philology you or your school perhaps prefer something more personal.

In the format of your bibliography, Word offers some convenient templates you can use. Note that even if you decide to use built-in templates, you can always customize their style. In any case the rule you won't like to ignore is that your readers should be able to follow your references easily, to discern at once authors and titles.

---

[21] Bibliographical 'styles' here is a technical term for academic standards of reference, not to be confused with Word's styles used elsewhere in a document.

If (even some of) your references need two or more lines, use hanging identation, letting your first line be prominent. Use also a comfortable line height, and an even greater distance from reference to reference.

Archer, Joanne Archer, Ann M. Hanlon, and Jennie A. Levine. "Investigating Primary Source Literacy." *Journal of Academic Librarianship* 35, no. 5 (September 2009): 410-420.

Barrett, Andy. "The Information-Seeking Habits of Graduate Student Researchers in the Humanities." *The Journal of Academic Librarianship* 31, no. 4 (July 2005): 324-331.

Cole, Charles. "Information Acquisition in History Ph.d. Students: Inferencing and the Formation of Knowledge Structures." *The Library Quarterly* 68, no. 1 (Jan., 1998): 33-54.

Daniel, Dominique. "Teaching Students how to Research the Past: Historians and Librarians in the Digital Age." *The History Teacher* 45, no. 2 (February 2012): 261-282.

Creating Indexes of persons or topics

Take some time (you don't need much) to mark important entries and create a useful Index.

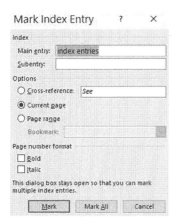

This dialogue lets you mark Index entries, and is convenient. Let's see a few less known details and some important settings you should care about to avoid problems with your Index.

Index Subentries

You insert a subentry when a reader would expect a specialized term under a general topic. For example, writing a book that mentions a lot the Windows OS, you may have Windows as a general term and create subentries for versions such as 7, 10, S, etc.

Subentries can have levels. To create *subentries of subentries*, separate them using a colon. For example, if your main entry is "OS", you can have a second and a third level subentry such as "Windows:S". This appears in your final Index like this:

```
OS
    Windows
            S, 53
```

Cross-references

Cross-references help a reader to find information elsewhere than expected.[22]

To use the previous example, if you believe that someone may browse your Index for a term like "Tablet Settings", you can create this Index entry as a starting point to send him to the "Tablets" subentry of your main "Windows" entry. A cross-reference with levels appears like this in your final Index:

```
Tablet Settings. See Windows > Tablets
```

---

[22] Don't confuse Index cross-references with *links* you can create to let yourself and other users of the *digital* document (not the print version) jump to specific parts of it or even to other documents. This link is created at the Insert > Cross-reference menu, while building an Index cross-reference is provided as a sub-option in the panel that lets you mark Index entries.

To create cross-reference levels, just add to an entry a symbol your reader will be able to understand, e.g. "Windows > Tablets".

Create cross-references only if your Index is really large and detailed, otherwise you introduce unnecessary distractions rather than help.

Time to build your Index!

> Contrary to basic font and page formatting, an Index should be among your very l a s t tasks.

Since you are going to revise your text several times, there is no point in creating Index entries for terms that may even be removed in the course of your project along with sentences or even whole paragraphs or pages where they belong.

The right time to mark Index entries is when you read your book for the final check, making only minor changes, if any.

Punctuation marks can make your life difficult as they keep altering natural sorting. There is nothing you can do about it, but only change these entries in a way that avoids punctuation marks.

For example, when "Einstein Studies" appears above "Einstein, Albert" because it lacks a punctuation mark, think about removing this comma after Einstein's name.

How to create more than one Index in the same document

How many Indexes do you need? Just one all-inclusive, or perhaps one for topics and one for persons, or one for places and one for monuments, etc.?

If they need indexing at all, most books are fine with a single Index, which may be the reason why adding entries for a second or even more Indexes is not supported by Word's *Mark Index Entry* panel: you have to work with *field codes*. It may seem a little tricky, but it's not difficult.

When you mark an Index entry, Word enters this "XE" code behind the scenes:

```
{XE "Some keyword"}
```

When you insert in your document the *list* of entries, that is the Index itself, Word uses this "INDEX" code:

```
{INDEX}
```

To view field codes in your document, press Ctrl+Shift+Asterisk[23]

---

[23] If you find it more convenient, you can use the Show/Hide ¶ toggle button at the Home ribbon.

Both codes, that of the entries and that of the Index, can be customized to become unique and support several specialized Indexes.

For instance, to create an Index for places and another one for monuments, you can modify the codes above adding an "f" switch.

For all the entries *of places*, use a field code like {XE "Boston" \f "1"}, and for the final Index of Places, use a code like {INDEX \f "1"}.

For all the entries *of monuments*, use a code like {XE "Bunker Hill" \f "2"}, and for the Index of Monuments, use a code like {INDEX \f "2"}.

As you notice in the examples above, *the f switch connects an Index with its entries and it must be identical*. A field code can have only one f switch. In our example, if you have a place and a monument with the exact same name, you need to create two Index entries.

In case that Index ID numbers (the f switch) confuse you, just add a description, for instance: *"1places", "2monuments"*. Word will stick to the first character, the ID number, and you take advantage of the rest to make sure you won't mark an entry for the wrong Index.

So far so good. Just a little caution and everything will be fine. The tedious part of creating those Indexes is the actual marking of your entries, since Word won't provide an option for that in the Marking Panel.

A solution is to add to your entries a unique sequence of digits and / or letters for each of your Indexes. When your work finishes, with nothing left but to build the Indexes, just use the Finder to replace each unique sequence with the code needed for Word to determine the ID of your entries.

For instance, when you create an entry for Boston using the Marking Panel, instead of writing just Boston, you can write Boston1places (1 is the ID of your Index of places). Word will create this code:

```
{XE "Boston1places"}
```

Doing the same for all your places, you have entries like, {XE "Boston1places"}, {XE "Los Angeles1places"}, {XE "New York1places"}, etc.

When you are ready to build your Indexes, *Find and Replace* those entries with the rest of the code that Word needs to identify your entries as belonging to a particular Index, in our example the Index "1", or Index of Places.

Press Ctrl+Shift+Asterisk to reveal the field codes, then search for

```
1places
```

and replace all instances of it with

```
" \f "1
```

This replacement code may seem incomprehensible, but if you pay attention you can understand its form. Let me explain it, in case you are confused.

Here is a complete entry of a place, including a temporary mark that helps you relate this entry with a particular Index:

```
{XE "Boston1places"}
```

The entry does not include the f switch that attaches it to the Index of Places, but you know where it belongs because the very keyword contains the temporary mark: *1places*, with "1" being the Index ID, and the word "places" functioning as a simple reminder for you.

If we add manually the *f switch*, which in our example is number "1", our entry becomes, {XE "Boston1places" \f "1"}.

As we now are going to build the Index, we don't need anymore the temporary mark "1places" but only the term "Boston". Therefore, for an automatic replacement of all instances in all keywords of Places, we need to search for *1places* and replace it with the rest of the code that makes up a functional entry of the Index of Places. Since the beginning of the entry is already as it should be, {XE "Boston, we search for *1places* to replace it with the ending of the field code

Field codes end in a quote and a bracket "} but in our Replace operation it seems like we left the code open. However, it won't remain open since the closing is already there and it won't be replaced:

From an entry like {XE "Boston1places"}, we don't keep only the start, which is {XE "Boston, but also the final quote and bracket "}, replacing only the reminder *1places* with the code that identifies this entry with the Index of Places.

In " \f "1 the first quotation mark closes the entry "Boston, then comes the \f switch "1 with one quotation mark only, since the other quotation mark is already there along with the ending bracket.

I hope now everything is clear, but

Before you make massive replacements, always create a backup of your document!

You can always use the undo function, but just in case something goes wrong, don't underestimate an extra safety measure to be certain you won't lose all those precious Index entries. Experiment a while to understand how such replacements work.

After you create the field codes of your Index entries, do not forget to add the f switch also to the codes of your Indexes, {INDEX \f "1"} and {INDEX \f "2"}.

First build an Index (at *References > Insert Index*), then 1) reveal its field code, 2) add the f switch, and 3) update the Index. Repeat the same steps for your second Index in a separate section of your document.

If your Index ignores your custom font style

You may have created an Index that won't obey its own style!, using instead a font family that differs from the one you explicitely defined.

To solve this problem, click first somewhere inside your Index and see the name of the style that the Index is supposed to use.[24] Right click on the style name to modify it and make sure that indeed the style of your Index uses the font that you like.

Now that you saw the name of the Index style, and you are also sure that your style is defined as you wish, select the entire Index, and click on the style name to apply this style to your Index.

Then *right* click on the Index itself and update it.

You may do all of this to find that your Index still refuses to display the font of your choice!

Place the cursor somewhere inside your Index to see what font is actually used by Word contrary to your adjustments.

Now check in the Control Panel the Fonts applet: is that font listed there? If not, you just found the reason of your trouble.

Install the missing font and Word will s t o p using it for your Index!

Obviously Word should use an alternative font even if you wouldn't care to define it yourself, instead of insisting on a ghost, but there is no such thing as a "perfect" program.

---

[24] If the style is not visible immediately, click the little arrow at the bottom right corner of the Styles section to open a larger list of styles.

Adding Pictures

Pictures can be sources of information and inspiration: do not hesitate to make use of them. You can drag and drop them in your text, or copy and paste them. You can also choose among the options included in Insert > Illustrations.

How to protect image quality

Before anything else, you need to make sure Word won't damage the quality of your graphics, especially if you are going to cooperate with a professional publisher.

Open Word's Options > Advanced, go to the *Image Size and Quality* section at the right, and select any resolution equal or greater than 300 ppi. You can disable compression, but even if you won't, Word will always respect the target resolution (ppi).

☑ Do not compress images in file ⓘ
Set default target output to: 330 ppi ▼

You have to draw, shoot or find high resolution images. Word —or any program—cannot 'upgrade' a low quality source, and while on screen your image may appear more than acceptable, don't be surprised if you find distortions in print.

How do you know the resolution of your images?

If you are on Windows Explorer right click on an image to open its Properties tab. Then go to *Details* and see the resolution. You can also find this information in most commercial or free image editors.

Cropping your images

Edit your images before you insert them in Word, if possible, since your specialized photo editor provides more accuracy and convenience, but you can also make exceptions and apply some changes from inside Word.

Cropping is a most useful function, especially when you prefer to discard immediately some portion in order for your image to fit the page without reducing a part of it that you consider important.

You can also use cropping in Word to instantly get rid of a border or some distortion, etc., avoiding to open a photo editor, retouch your image and import it again in the document.

Cropping is available when you select an image and go to Picture tools or right click on it. When your image is too large, a particular edge may not even be visible, which means you cannot crop it!

Just resort to the *Format Picture* dialogue that you get when you right click your image.

In the "Picture" tab select how many pixels you'd like cropped from whatever side.

You can keep cropping your image this way until it becomes entirely visible, letting you use the more convenient drag and drop cropping. Or you can drag and drop it at the opposite direction to hide temporarily a part of it that you don't need to edit, and let the other part show up.

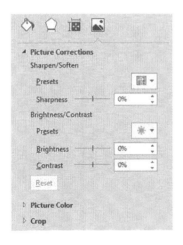

Word lets you also change brightness, contrast, saturation, and much more, which you can try. If you are not satisfied, use your regular image editor, and reinsert you picture.

You can also use *compression* to reduce the size of your document, provided you leave intact the resolution of all images, if you are going to print.

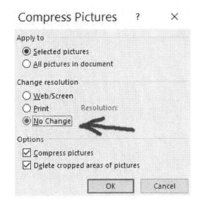

The "Size" tab of the "Size and Position (Layout)" dialogue contains some self evident adjustments I won't talk about, and one that is particularly important.

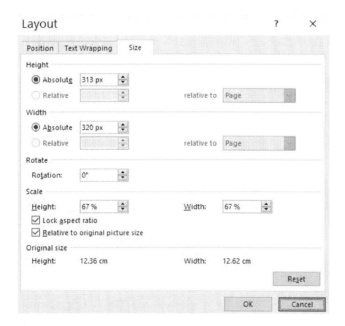

Watch the "Scale" section, where it says "67%". This means your image is much larger than what you actually want and use of it!

If your document contains a lot of images in such a scale, it will be unnecessarily heavy. Try to use images of dimensions that remain close to 100% after you insert them in Word. Unless, of course, you don't care for your document's size.

Certain publishers have a size limit in documents they will accept. Amazon's CreateSpace won't allow your document to be larger than 400 MB. It is generous, but wait until you have a full color coffee table book containing high quality images…

Inserting Excel Objects

Nothing easier! Just copy your chart from Excel and paste it anywhere in Word using the Paste Special > P a s t e   L i n k option.

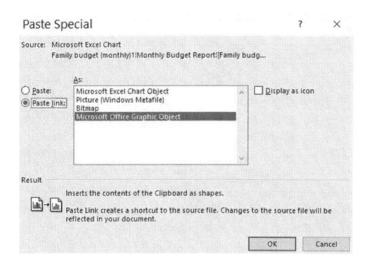

Don't forget that you can also use Word itself for your charts, in case you haven't already built them in Excel.

To create a chart in Word, go to Insert > Chart.

Publish!

The joy of an author is conception, expression, understanding, completion and sharing! You wouldn't like to betray so much effort, hope and delight preparing your document for the printer. Printing is easy enough, but some aspects of it may not be that obvious.

Contents of this section

How to check your document for errors	109
Making temporary home prints in various paper sizes	111
How to compare two documents	112
How to create a PDF version for professional publishers	114
Word and Acrobat paper size problems	116
How to insert and resize an image in Acrobat	117
Checking your final PDF for errors	117

How to check your document for errors

To be effective you need to check your document for errors several times. It would also help a lot to divide your job in specialized tasks. For instance, first check your grammar, then your syntax, then layout, then your graphics, etc. Checking one thing at a time helps to keep focus and prevents oversights.

> Especially when you check your grammar you may need to apply a high level zoom to make sure you won't skip errors.

Word checks spelling well, missing often the context, the meaning of a word as you intend it, and accepts a form that is correct only in a different context and use. For instance, if I write *you car* instead of *your car*, Word won't find the spelling error! You need to be careful even in sentences that aren't marked by Word for errors.

If you avoid using always the same words, trying to find some nuances, Word's S y n o n y m s can help. Right clicking on a word and going to *synonyms*, you find also *antonyms*, if the program is able to provide some for a word.[25] To ignore subtle differences is not strictly speaking an "error", but a serious weakness and a possible cause of misunderstandings.

---

[25] Synonym comes from the Greek *syn* (=along with) + *onoma* (=name), antonym from *anti* (=opposite) + *onoma*.

As you search for errors, you may need to locate something in several pages, just to make sure it is there or to replace it, etc.

There is a feature in Word that may become annoying.

After you find what you was searching for using the Finder, you hit escape to start working on the page that contains the keyword(s) you just found, but, instead of that, Word brings you back to the point where your cursor was before you started to search!

To avoid losing the current page, do not hit escape: you have to first hit Enter, then Escape! This way Word won't change page, Escape just gives focus on the particular search result you was viewing when you pressed Enter.

There is also your familiar "Advanced Find"…

Ctrl+F opens the navigation bar at the left of the document. The main advantage of this way is that you can see immediately (if your search results are not too many) your keyword in context.

If you don't like this default function, preferring to use Advanced Find, here is what you can do.

Go to Word Options > Customize Ribbon > Keyboard Shortcuts > Customize > All Commands > EditFind. In the *Press new shortcut key* box write Ctrl+F or whatever combination you prefer. Assign it and press OK.

To use also the Navigation Pane whenever you want, you can assign a keyboard shortcut to that function too. Locate the *NavPaneSearch* command and associate it with any shortcut you like.

When you perform a search and there exist many occurrences of your term, you don't need to find them using the main Find Dialogue — in the navigation bar or not. You can close the Finder to reclaim space and jump to the next occurrence immediately by pressing Shift + F4, or Ctrl + Alt + Y.[26]

Making temporary home prints in various paper sizes

Let's say you have a 6" × 9" document or even smaller, but you need a copy from your home printer, using A4 paper, to check for errors without using your screen, to give it to a friend, or for any other reason.

Of course, you want to keep intact the original layout of your document, even if your margins seem huge in A4.

Just let Word "scale" your document to paper size. You will find this option in File > Print > Settings.

At the bottom, where it reads "1 page per sheet", click and select "Scale to paper size", then just pick A4, or any size you will be using for your temporary print jobs:

---

[26] If you prefer to change the "Find Again" shortcut to, e.g., F3, go to Options > Customize the Ribbon > Keyboard Shortcuts. Locate the "All Commands" option at the left, and then the RepeatFind command at the right.

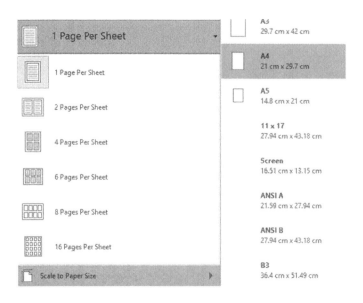

Another easy way out would be to save your document in PDF format and let Acrobat print it.

Adobe lets you select a paper size different than the size of your document's page setup and it will even let you preview the results. Enjoy your document occupying the center of the larger A4 size, and go on with printing!

How to compare two documents

If you need to compare two or more versions of your document, you don't have to use specialized applications, Word itself gives enough help. Go to Review > Compare > Compare, to select your documents and the way you'd like the differences presented.

Just experiment and decide on the final Word's option of viewing the differences in a new document or not. To select your documents you may prefer to use this folder icon at the right of the Drop Down menu, because it lets you find them in Windows Explorer.[27]

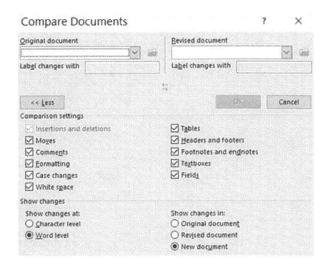

If you are after specific changes and differences, press the "More" button to reveal more options, and clear any of them that may produce more results than you need — *uncheck* "Case changes", "Comments", or anything you are not interested in at the moment.

The same for the right column of options. If you try to locate differences only in your footnotes, clear the rest and keep only the Footnotes / Endnotes option.

---

[27] The Drop Down menus of this panel contain a lot of options that can be confusing.

How to create a PDF version for professional publishers

Publishers such as Amazon's CreateSpace prefer a PDF version of a document.[28] They accept Word formats (doc, docx, even rtf), warning that *print-ready PDF files created through desktop publishing software offer the most control over the appearance of your book.*

It's true. Although a PDF version cannot be better than its source, the Word document itself may change, even according to the printer used. Remember what was said above, at the "page metrics" chapter?

Printing a Word document may also be influenced by particular configurations of the operating system and Office. PDF is like a realistic photo, it cannot become better than its subject, it won't become worse either.

---

[28] You won't find a lot of difficulties in cooperating with CreateSpace. The rules are clear, help abundant, a community of users, simplicity all the way! Some problems exist though; you cannot have hard cover editions, you cannot select the quality of interior or cover papers, you cannot have a few colorful pages in an otherwise black and white book, there is no sewing binding if you don't like glue... Let's hope some or all of this changes in the future, but even with problems CreateSpace remains a great option, if you prefer publishing on demand. Just make sure you prepare a quality PDF version of your work.

Are there any serious difficulties that you need to overcome trying to achieve a PDF quality that won't disappoint your publisher and your readers?

First thing to know: If you let Word create your PDF, prefer the *Save As* option instead of Print > Microsoft Print to PDF. By *Saving as* you are given the chance to adjust more settings, even avoid the risk of ending up with a faulty page size!

I assume of course that you've already followed this advice,[29] upon *creating* a new document, to *immediately* enable the highest resolution settings for your images — no less than 300 ppi.

To control even more options and go for the highest PDF quality, your best bet is Adobe Acrobat. In this case, the moment you create your document and begin to think basic configuration, such as paper size and margins, you need to go to *Print* and select Adobe PDF as your printer. Then go to Printer Properties and select Press Quality. This setting is enough, but you can tweak it further according to the requirements of your publisher.

You cannot create your book's cover in Word, or Acrobat; for this you need programs like Adobe inDesign or Microsoft Publisher.[30] Just measure well the spine and bleeds. This is all the technical difficulty you will really find, the rest being matters of taste, culture, and some exercise.

---

[29] *Cf.* Adding pictures > Image quality.

[30] Especially when it comes to Covers, Publisher doesn't hold a candle to inDesign! If you have the chance go for it, without a second thought.

Word and Acrobat paper size problems

When it prints a document as PDF, Acrobat may ignore the paper size specified in Word. In Printing Preferences it lets you define the "Adobe PDF Page Size". Why then this printing job ends to a different size, than what you selected in Acrobat itself?

It doesn't seem to matter a lot how the "Adobe PDF Page Size" is configured in Printing Preferences, when this adjustment differs from what is provided in the Default Settings!

To print your document as you want it, go to Acrobat's Default Settings, edit your custom size, and define there what is used in your Word document. Acrobat obeys this setting, no matter what you select in "Adobe PDF Page Size".

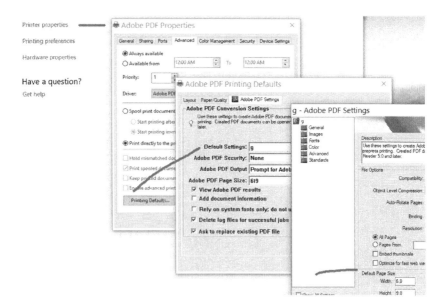

How to insert and resize an image in Acrobat

You just printed your document to realize that you'd like this image replaced! Is there any way to do that directly on your PDF version, instead or replacing the image in Word and then reprinting the Word document as PDF?

It might seem but it's not difficult to insert an image in a PDF document. Right click anywhere and select the *Add image* command. You can also customize Acrobat's toolbar to add there this command, if you right click on it and go to *Customize Quick Tools*.

After your image is imported you can click on it to place it anywhere you like. If it's too large, resize it. You can also use the "Edit" command to select a picture, then use Acrobat's "Replace Image" button to replace an image with another one you can choose.

Checking your final PDF for errors

So much effort comes to a glorious end in this PDF you are going to submit to your publisher! Especially when you edit and preview in Acrobat the final form of your work, you may like to have odd pages at the right, which is how a book is read. Acrobat, even in *two pages* view, starts with the first page at the left, showing even pages at the right!

To browse your document like a real book, go to View > Page Display, and select the option *Show Cover Page in Two Page View*.

To do the same in Word, at Page Setup select *mirror margins*, and your problem is solved.

Appendix: Word Keyboard Shortcuts

Some of the most useful shortcuts you may not be familiar with. Don't neglect them: they will make your life in Word a lot easier. Dedicate some time each day to read and learn.

Go to "Tell me what you want to do" (Command Search)	Alt+Q
Decrease font size 1 point	Ctrl+[
Increase font size 1 point	Ctrl+]
Re-do	Ctrl+Y
Zoom	Alt+W, Q, then tab in Zoom dialog box to the value you want.

Navigate the ribbon with only the keyboard

To go to the ribbon, press Alt, and then, to move between tabs, use the Right Arrow and Left Arrow keys. To go directly to a specific tab on the ribbon, use one of the following access keys (you don't need to learn them by heart since they appear when you press Alt):

To use Backstage view, open the File page.	Alt+F
To use themes, colors, and effects, such as page borders, open the Design tab.	Alt+G
To use common formatting commands, paragraph styles, or to use the Find tool, open Home tab.	Alt+H

To manage Mail Merge tasks, or to work with envelopes and labels, open Mailings tab.	Alt+M
To insert tables, pictures and shapes, headers, or text boxes, open Insert tab.	Alt+N
To work with page margins, page orientation, indentation, and spacing, open Layout tab.	Alt+P
To type a search term for Help content, open "Tell me" box on ribbon.	Alt+Q, then enter the search term
To use Spell Check, set proofing languages, or to track and review changes to your document, open the Review tab.	Alt+R
To add a table of contents, footnotes, or a table of citations, open the References tab.	Alt+S
To choose a document view or mode, such as Read Mode or Outline view, open the View tab. You can also set Zoom magnification and manage multiple windows of documents.	Alt+W

To move between commands, press the Tab key or Shift+Tab.

To move in the group that's currently selected, press the Down Arrow key.

To move between groups on a ribbon, press Ctrl+Right Arrow or Ctrl+Left Arrow.

Controls on the ribbon are activated in different ways, depending upon the type of control:

If the selected command is a button, to activate it, press Spacebar or Enter.

If the selected command is a split button (that is, a button that opens a menu of additional options), to activate it, press Alt+Down Arrow. Tab through the options. To select the current option, press Spacebar or Enter.

> If the selected command is a list (such as the Font list), to open the list, press the Down Arrow key. Then, to move between items, use the Up Arrow or Down Arrow key.
>
> If the selected command is a gallery, to select the command, press Spacebar or Enter. Then, tab through the items.

In galleries with more than one row of items, the Tab key moves from the beginning to the end of the current row and, when it reaches the end of the row, it moves to the beginning of the next one. Pressing the Right Arrow key at the end of the current row moves back to the beginning of the current row.

Use access keys when you can see the KeyTips

To use access keys:

> Press Alt, then press the letter shown in the square KeyTip that appears over the ribbon command that you want to use.

Depending on which letter you press, you may be shown additional KeyTips, which are small images of a letter next to a command button on the tab that you picked. For example, if you press Alt+F, the Office Backstage opens on the Info page which has a different set of KeyTips. If you then press Alt again, KeyTips for navigating on this page appear.

Change the keyboard focus by using the keyboard without using the mouse

The following table lists some ways to move the keyboard focus when using only the keyboard.

Select the active tab of the ribbon and activate the access keys.	Alt or F10. Use access keys or arrow keys to move to a different tab.
Move the focus to commands on the ribbon.	Tab or Shift+Tab
Move the focus to each command on the ribbon, forward or backward, respectively.	Tab or Shift+Tab

Move down, up, left, or right, respectively, among the items on the ribbon.	Down Arrow, Up Arrow, Left Arrow, or Right Arrow
Expand or collapse the ribbon.	Ctrl+F1
Display the shortcut (context) menu for a selected item.	Shift+F10
Move the focus to a different pane of the window, such as the Format Picture pane, the Grammar pane, or the Selection pane.	F6
Activate a selected command or control on the ribbon.	Spacebar or Enter
Open a selected menu or gallery on the ribbon.	Spacebar or Enter
Finish modifying a value in a control on the ribbon, and move focus back to the document.	Enter

Create, view, and save documents

Create a new document.	Ctrl+N
Open a document.	Ctrl+O
Close a document.	Ctrl+W
Split the document window.	Alt+Ctrl+S
Remove the document window split.	Alt+Shift+C or Alt+Ctrl+S
Save a document.	Ctrl+S

Print and preview documents

Print a document.	Ctrl+P
Switch to print preview.	Alt+Ctrl+I
Move around the preview page when zoomed in.	Arrow keys

Check spelling and review changes in a document

Insert a comment (in the Revision task pane).	Alt+R, C
Turn change tracking on or off.	Ctrl+Shift+E
Close the Reviewing Pane if it is open.	Alt+Shift+C
Select Review tab on ribbon.	Alt+R, then Down Arrow to move to commands on this tab.
Select Spelling & Grammar	Alt+R, S

Find, replace, and go to specific items in the document

Open the search box in the Navigation task pane.	Ctrl+F
Replace text, specific formatting, and special items.	Ctrl+H
Go to a page, bookmark, footnote, table, comment, graphic, or other location.	Ctrl+G
Switch between the last four places that you have edited.	Alt+Ctrl+Z

Move around in a document using the keyboard

To the top of the window	Alt+Ctrl+Page Up
To the end of the window	Alt+Ctrl+Page Down
To the top of the next page	Ctrl+Page Down
To the top of the previous page	Ctrl+Page Up
To a previous revision	Shift+F5
After opening a document, to the location you were working in when the document was last closed	Shift+F5

Insert or mark Table of Contents, footnotes, and citations

Mark a table of contents entry.	Alt+Shift+O
Mark a table of authorities entry (citation).	Alt+Shift+I
Mark an index entry.	Alt+Shift+X
Insert a footnote.	Alt+Ctrl+F
Insert an endnote.	Alt+Ctrl+D
Go to next footnote.	Alt+Shift+>
Go to previous footnote.	Alt+Shift+<
Go to "Tell me what you want to do" and Smart Lookup.	Alt+Q

Work with documents in different views

Switch to Read Mode view	Alt+W, F
Switch to Print Layout view.	Alt+Ctrl+P
Switch to Outline view.	Alt+Ctrl+O
Switch to Draft view.	Alt+Ctrl+N

Work with headings in Outline view

Promote a paragraph.	Alt+Shift+Left Arrow
Demote a paragraph.	Alt+Shift+Right Arrow
Demote to body text.	Ctrl+Shift+N
Move selected paragraphs up.	Alt+Shift+Up Arrow
Move selected paragraphs down.	Alt+Shift+Down Arrow
Expand text under a heading.	Alt+Shift+Plus Sign
Collapse text under a heading.	Alt+Shift+Minus Sign
Expand or collapse all text or headings.	Alt+Shift+A
Hide or display character formatting.	The slash (/) key on the numeric keypad
Show the first line of text or all text.	Alt+Shift+L
Show all headings with the Heading 1 style.	Alt+Shift+1
Show all headings up to Heading n.	Alt+Shift+n
Insert a tab character.	Ctrl+Tab

Navigate in Read Mode view

Go to beginning of document.	Home
Go to end of document.	End
Go to page n.	n (n is the page number you want to go to), Enter
Exit Read mode.	Esc

Edit and move text and graphics

Extend a selection

Turn extend mode on.	F8
Select the nearest character.	F8, and then press Left Arrow or Right Arrow
Increase the size of a selection.	F8 (press once to select a word, twice to select a sentence, and so on)
Reduce the size of a selection.	Shift+F8
Turn extend mode off.	Esc
Extend a selection one character to the right.	Shift+Right Arrow
Extend a selection one character to the left.	Shift+Left Arrow
Extend a selection to the end of a word.	Ctrl+Shift+Right Arrow
Extend a selection to the beginning of a word.	Ctrl+Shift+Left Arrow
Extend a selection to the end of a line.	Shift+End

Extend a selection to the beginning of a line.	Shift+Home
Extend a selection one line down.	Shift+Down Arrow
Extend a selection one line up.	Shift+Up Arrow
Extend a selection to the end of a paragraph.	Ctrl+Shift+Down Arrow
Extend a selection to the beginning of a paragraph.	Ctrl+Shift+Up Arrow
Extend a selection one screen down.	Shift+Page Down
Extend a selection one screen up.	Shift+Page Up
Extend a selection to the beginning of a document.	Ctrl+Shift+Home
Extend a selection to the end of a document.	Ctrl+Shift+End
Extend a selection to the end of a window.	Alt+Ctrl+Shift+Page Down
Extend a selection to include the entire document.	Ctrl+A
Select a vertical block of text.	Ctrl+Shift+F8, and then use the arrow keys; press Esc to cancel selection mode
Extend a selection to a specific location in a document.	F8+arrow keys; press Esc to cancel selection mode

Delete text and graphics

Delete one word to the left.	Ctrl+Backspace
Delete one word to the right.	Ctrl+Delete

Cut to the Spike. (Spike is a feature that allows you to collect groups of text from different locations and paste them in another location).	Ctrl+F3

Copy and move text and graphics

Open the Office Clipboard	Press Alt+H to move to the Home tab, and then press F,O.
Move text or graphics once.	F2 (then move the cursor and press Enter)
Copy text or graphics once.	Shift+F2 (then move the cursor and press Enter)
When text or an object is selected, open the Create New Building Block dialog box.	Alt+F3
When the building block — for example, a SmartArt graphic — is selected, display the shortcut menu that is associated with it.	Shift+F10
Cut to the Spike.	Ctrl+F3
Paste the Spike contents.	Ctrl+Shift+F3
Copy the header or footer used in the previous section of the document.	Alt+Shift+R

Edit and navigate tables

Select text and graphics in a table

Select the next cell's contents.	Tab
Select the preceding cell's contents.	Shift+Tab
Extend a selection to adjacent cells.	Hold down Shift and press an arrow key repeatedly
Select a column.	Use the arrow keys to move to the column's top or bottom cell, and then do one of the following:
Press Shift+Alt+Page Down to select the column from top to bottom.	Press Shift+Alt+Page Up to select the column from bottom to top.
Select an entire row	Use arrow keys to move to end of the row, either the first cell (leftmost) in the row or to the last cell (rightmost) in the row.
From the first cell in the row, press Shift+Alt+End to select the row from left to right.	From the last cell in the row, press Shift+Alt+Home to select the row from right to left.
Extend a selection (or block).	Ctrl+Shift+F8, and then use the arrow keys; press Esc to cancel selection mode
Select an entire table.	Alt+5 on the numeric keypad (with Num Lock off)

Move around in a table

To the next cell in a row	Tab
To the previous cell in a row	Shift+Tab

To the first cell in a row	Alt+Home
To the last cell in a row	Alt+End
To the first cell in a column	Alt+Page Up
To the last cell in a column	Alt+Page Down
To the previous row	Up Arrow
To the next row	Down Arrow
Row up	Alt+Shift+Up Arrow
Row down	Alt+Shift+Down Arrow

Insert paragraphs and tab characters in a table

New paragraphs in a cell	Enter
Tab characters in a cell	Ctrl+Tab

Format characters and paragraphs

Format characters

Open the Font dialog box to change the formatting of characters.	Ctrl+D
Change the case of letters.	Shift+F3
Format all letters as capitals.	Ctrl+Shift+A
Apply bold formatting.	Ctrl+B
Apply an underline.	Ctrl+U
Underline words but not spaces.	Ctrl+Shift+W
Double-underline text.	Ctrl+Shift+D

Apply hidden text formatting.	Ctrl+Shift+H
Apply italic formatting.	Ctrl+I
Format letters as small capitals.	Ctrl+Shift+K
Apply subscript formatting (automatic spacing).	Ctrl+Equal Sign
Apply superscript formatting (automatic spacing).	Ctrl+Shift+Plus Sign
Remove manual character formatting.	Ctrl+Spacebar
Change the selection to the Symbol font.	Ctrl+Shift+Q

Change or re-size the font

Open the Font dialog box to change the font.	Ctrl+Shift+F
Increase the font size.	Ctrl+Shift+>
Decrease the font size.	Ctrl+Shift+<
Increase the font size by 1 point.	Ctrl+]
Decrease the font size by 1 point.	Ctrl+[

Copy formatting

Copy formatting from text.	Ctrl+Shift+C
Apply copied formatting to text.	Ctrl+Shift+V

Change paragraph alignment

Switch a paragraph between centered and left-aligned.	Ctrl+E
Switch a paragraph between justified and left-aligned.	Ctrl+J
Switch a paragraph between right-aligned and left-aligned.	Ctrl+R
Left align a paragraph.	Ctrl+L
Indent a paragraph from the left.	Ctrl+M
Remove a paragraph indent from the left.	Ctrl+Shift+M
Create a hanging indent.	Ctrl+T
Reduce a hanging indent.	Ctrl+Shift+T
Remove paragraph formatting.	Ctrl+Q

Copy and review text formats

Display nonprinting characters.	Ctrl+Shift+* (asterisk on numeric keypad does not work)
Review text formatting.	Shift+F1 (then click the text with the formatting you want to review)
Copy formats.	Ctrl+Shift+C
Paste formats.	Ctrl+Shift+V

Set line spacing

Single-space lines.	Ctrl+1
Double-space lines.	Ctrl+2
Set 1.5-line spacing.	Ctrl+5
Add or remove one line space preceding a paragraph.	Ctrl+0 (zero)

Apply Styles to paragraphs

Open Apply Styles task pane.	Ctrl+Shift+S
Open Styles task pane.	Alt+Ctrl+Shift+S
Start AutoFormat.	Alt+Ctrl+K
Apply the Normal style.	Ctrl+Shift+N
Apply the Heading 1 style.	Alt+Ctrl+1
Apply the Heading 2 style.	Alt+Ctrl+2
Apply the Heading 3 style.	Alt+Ctrl+3

To close the Styles task pane

    If the Styles task pane is not selected, press F6 to select it.

    Press Ctrl+Spacebar.

    Use the arrow keys to select Close, and then press Enter.

Insert special characters

A field	Ctrl+F9
A line break	Shift+Enter
A page break	Ctrl+Enter
A column break	Ctrl+Shift+Enter
An em dash	Alt+Ctrl+Minus Sign (on the numeric keypad)
An en dash	Ctrl+Minus Sign (on the numeric keypad)
An optional hyphen	Ctrl+Hyphen
A nonbreaking hyphen	Ctrl+Shift+Hyphen
A nonbreaking space	Ctrl+Shift+Spacebar
The copyright symbol	Alt+Ctrl+C
The registered trademark symbol	Alt+Ctrl+R
The trademark symbol	Alt+Ctrl+T
An ellipsis	Alt+Ctrl+Period
A single opening quotation mark	Ctrl+`(single quotation mark), `(single quotation mark)
A single closing quotation mark	Ctrl+' (single quotation mark), ' (single quotation mark)
Double opening quotation marks	Ctrl+` (single quotation mark), Shift+' (single quotation mark)
Double closing quotation marks	Ctrl+' (single quotation mark), Shift+' (single quotation mark)
An AutoText entry	Enter (after you type the first few characters of the AutoText entry name and when the ScreenTip appears)

Insert characters by using character codes

Insert the Unicode character for the specified Unicode (hexadecimal) character code. For example, to insert the euro currency symbol (€), type 20AC, and then hold down Alt and press X.	The character code, Alt+X
Find out the Unicode character code for the selected character	Alt+X
Insert the ANSI character for the specified ANSI (decimal) character code. For example, to insert the euro currency symbol, hold down Alt and press 0128 on the numeric keypad.	Alt+the character code (on the numeric keypad)

Insert and edit objects

Insert an object

>Press Alt, N, J, and then J to open the Object dialog box.
>
>Do one of the following.
>
>>Press Down Arrow to select an object type, and then press Enter to create an object.
>>
>>Press Ctrl+Tab to switch to the Create from File tab, press Tab, and then type the file name of the object that you want to insert or browse to the file.

Edit an object

>With the cursor positioned to the left of the object in your document, select the object by pressing Shift+Right Arrow.
>
>Press Shift+F10.
>
>Press the Tab key to get to Object name, press Enter, and then press Enter again.

Insert SmartArt graphics

> Press and release Alt, N, and then M to select SmartArt.
>
> Press the arrow keys to select the type of graphic that you want.
>
> Press Tab, and then press the arrow keys to select the graphic that you want to insert.
>
> Press Enter.

Insert WordArt

> Press and release Alt, N, and then W to select WordArt.
>
> Press the arrow keys to select the WordArt style that you want, and then press Enter.
>
> Type the text that you want.
>
> Press Esc to select the WordArt object, and then use the arrow keys to move the object.
>
> Press Esc again to return to return to the document.

Mail merge and fields

Note: You must press Alt+M, or click Mailings, to use these keyboard shortcuts.

Work with fields

Insert a DATE field.	Alt+Shift+D
Insert a LISTNUM field.	Alt+Ctrl+L
Insert a Page field.	Alt+Shift+P
Insert a TIME field.	Alt+Shift+T
Insert an empty field.	Ctrl+F9
Update linked information in a Microsoft Word source document.	Ctrl+Shift+F7

Update selected fields.	F9
Unlink a field.	Ctrl+Shift+F9
Switch between a selected field code and its result.	Shift+F9
Switch between all field codes and their results.	Alt+F9
Run GOTOBUTTON or MACROBUTTON from the field that displays the field results.	Alt+Shift+F9
Go to the next field.	F11
Go to the previous field.	Shift+F11
Lock a field.	Ctrl+F11
Unlock a field.	Ctrl+Shift+F11

Set proofing language

If your document contains words or phrases in a different language than the default, it's a good idea to set the proofing language for those words. This not only makes it possible to check spelling and grammar for those phrases, it makes it possible for assistive technologies like screen readers to handle them.

Open the Set Proofing Language dialog box	Alt+R, U, L
Review list of proofing languages	Down Arrow
Set default languages	Alt+R, L

Turn on East Asian Input Method Editors

Turn Japanese Input Method Editor (IME) on 101 keyboard on or off.	Alt+~
Turn Korean Input Method Editor (IME) on 101 keyboard on or off.	Right Alt
Turn Chinese Input Method Editor (IME) on 101 keyboard on or off.	Ctrl+Spacebar

Function key reference

Get Help or visit Office.com.	F1
Move text or graphics.	F2
Repeat the last action.	F4
Choose the Go To command (Home tab).	F5
Go to the next pane or frame.	F6
Choose the Spelling command (Review tab).	F7
Extend a selection.	F8
Update the selected fields.	F9
Show KeyTips.	F10
Go to the next field.	F11
Choose the Save As command.	F12

Shift+Function keys

Start context-sensitive Help or reveal formatting.	Shift+F1
Copy text.	Shift+F2
Change the case of letters.	Shift+F3
Repeat a Find or Go To action.	Shift+F4
Move to the last change.	Shift+F5
Go to the previous pane or frame (after pressing F6).	Shift+F6
Choose the Thesaurus command (Review tab, Proofing group).	Shift+F7
Reduce the size of a selection.	Shift+F8
Switch between a field code and its result.	Shift+F9
Display a shortcut menu.	Shift+F10
Go to the previous field.	Shift+F11
Choose the Save command.	Shift+F12

Ctrl+Function keys

Expand or collapse the ribbon.	Ctrl+F1
Choose the Print Preview command.	Ctrl+F2
Cut to the Spike.	Ctrl+F3
Close the window.	Ctrl+F4
Go to the next window.	Ctrl+F6
Insert an empty field.	Ctrl+F9

Maximize the document window.	Ctrl+F10
Lock a field.	Ctrl+F11
Choose the Open command.	Ctrl+F12

Ctrl+Shift+Function keys

Insert the contents of the Spike.	Ctrl+Shift+F3
Edit a bookmark.	Ctrl+Shift+F5
Go to the previous window.	Ctrl+Shift+F6
Update linked information in a Word source document.	Ctrl+Shift+F7
Extend a selection or block.	Ctrl+Shift+F8, and then press an arrow key
Unlink a field.	Ctrl+Shift+F9
Unlock a field.	Ctrl+Shift+F11
Choose the Print command.	Ctrl+Shift+F12

Alt+Function keys

Go to the next field.	Alt+F1
Create a new Building Block.	Alt+F3
Exit Word.	Alt+F4
Restore the program window size.	Alt+F5
Move from an open dialog box back to the document, for dialog boxes that support this behavior.	Alt+F6

Find the next misspelling or grammatical error.	Alt+F7
Run a macro.	Alt+F8
Switch between all field codes and their results.	Alt+F9
Display the Selection task pane.	Alt+F10
Display Microsoft Visual Basic code.	Alt+F11

Alt+Shift+Function keys

Go to the previous field.	Alt+Shift+F1
Choose the Save command.	Alt+Shift+F2
Run GOTOBUTTON or MACROBUTTON from the field that displays the field results.	Alt+Shift+F9
Display a menu or message for an available action.	Alt+Shift+F10
Choose Table of Contents button in the Table of Contents container when the container is active.	Alt+Shift+F12

THEFREEWINDOWS

www.TheFreeWindows.com

Made in the USA
Monee, IL
26 January 2020